WILLIAM SHAKESPEARE was born in Stratford-upon-Avon in April, 1564, and his birth is traditionally celebrated on April 23. The facts of his life, known from surviving documents, are sparse. He was one of eight children born to John Shakespeare, a merchant of some standing in his community. William probably went to the King's New School in Stratford, but he had no university education. In November 1582, at the age of eighteen, he married Anne Hathaway, eight years his senior, who was pregnant with their first child, Susanna. She was born on May 26, 1583. Twins, a boy, Hamnet (who would die at age eleven), and a girl, Judith, were born in 1585. By 1592 Shakespeare had gone to London, working as an actor and already known as a playwright. A rival dramatist, Robert Greene, referred to him as "an upstart crow, beautified with our feathers." Shakespeare became a principal shareholder and playwright of the successful acting troupe the Lord Chamberlain's men (later, under James I, called the King's men). In 1599 the Lord Chamberlain's men built and occupied the Globe Theatre in Southwark near the Thames River. Here many of Shakespeare's plays were performed by the most famous actors of his time, including Richard Burbage, Will Kempe, and Robert Armin. In addition to his 37 plays, Shakespeare had a hand in others, including *Sir Thomas More* and *The Two Noble Kinsmen*, and he wrote poems, including *Venus and Adonis* and *The Rape of Lucrece*. His 154 sonnets were published, probably without his authorization, in 1609. In 1611 or 1612 he gave up his lodgings in London and devoted more and more of his time to retirement in Stratford, though he continued writing such plays as *The Tempest* and *Henry VIII* until about 1613. He died on April 23, 1616, and was buried in Holy Trinity Church, Stratford. No collected edition of his plays was published during his lifetime, but in 1623 two members of his acting company, John Heminges and Henry Condell, published the great collection now called the First Folio.

**Bantam Shakespeare
The Complete Works—29 Volumes
Edited by David Bevington
With forewords by Joseph Papp on the plays**

The Poems: Venus and Adonis, The Rape of Lucrece, The
Phoenix and Turtle, A Lover's Complaint,
the Sonnets

Antony and Cleopatra	*The Merchant of Venice*
As You Like It	*A Midsummer Night's Dream*
The Comedy of Errors	*Much Ado about Nothing*
Hamlet	*Othello*
Henry IV, Part One	*Richard II*
Henry IV, Part Two	*Richard III*
Henry V	*Romeo and Juliet*
Julius Caesar	*The Taming of the Shrew*
King Lear	*The Tempest*
Macbeth	*Twelfth Night*

Together in one volume:

Henry VI, Parts One, Two, and Three
King John and Henry VIII
*Measure for Measure, All's Well that Ends Well, and
     Troilus and Cressida*
Three Early Comedies: Love's Labor's Lost, The Two
                        Gentlemen of Verona, The Merry
                        Wives of Windsor
Three Classical Tragedies: Titus Andronicus, Timon
                             of Athens, Coriolanus
The Late Romances: Pericles, Cymbeline, The Winter's
                     Tale, The Tempest

Two collections:

Four Comedies: The Taming of the Shrew, A Midsummer
                 Night's Dream, The Merchant of Venice,
                 Twelfth Night
Four Tragedies: Hamlet, Othello, King Lear, Macbeth

William Shakespeare

MACBETH

Edited by
David Bevington

David Scott Kastan,
James Hammersmith,
and Robert Kean Turner,
Associate Editors

With a Foreword by
Joseph Papp

BANTAM BOOKS
NEW YORK · TORONTO · LONDON · SYDNEY · AUCKLAND

MACBETH

*A Bantam Book / published by arrangement
with Scott, Foresman and Company*

PUBLISHING HISTORY

*Scott, Foresman edition published / January 1980
Bantam edition, with newly edited text and substantially revised,
edited, and amplified notes, introductions, and other
materials, published / February 1988
Valuable advice on staging matters has been
provided by Richard Hosley.
Collations checked by Eric Rasmussen.
Additional editorial assistance by Claire McEachern.*

ISBN 0-553-21298-2

Published simultaneously in the United States and Canada

*Bantam Books are published by Bantam Books, a division of Bantam Doubleday Dell
Publishing Group, Inc. Its trademark, consisting of the words "Bantam Books" and the
portrayal of a rooster, is Registered in U.S. Patent and Trademark Office and in other
countries. Marca Registrada. Bantam Books, 1540 Broadway, New York, New York
10036.*

PRINTED IN THE UNITED STATES OF AMERICA

OPM   20 19 18 17 16 15 14 13 12 11 10

Contents

Foreword

It's hard to imagine, but Shakespeare wrote all of his plays with a quill pen, a goose feather whose hard end had to be sharpened frequently. How many times did he scrape the dull end to a point with his knife, dip it into the inkwell, and bring up, dripping wet, those wonderful words and ideas that are known all over the world?

In the age of word processors, typewriters, and ballpoint pens, we have almost forgotten the meaning of the word "blot." Yet when I went to school, in the 1930s, my classmates and I knew all too well what an inkblot from the metal-tipped pens we used would do to a nice clean page of a test paper, and we groaned whenever a splotch fell across the sheet. Most of us finished the school day with ink-stained fingers; those who were less careful also went home with ink-stained shirts, which were almost impossible to get clean.

When I think about how long it took me to write the simplest composition with a metal-tipped pen and ink, I can only marvel at how many plays Shakespeare scratched out with his goose-feather quill pen, year after year. Imagine him walking down one of the narrow cobblestoned streets of London, or perhaps drinking a pint of beer in his local alehouse. Suddenly his mind catches fire with an idea, or a sentence, or a previously elusive phrase. He is burning with impatience to write it down—but because he doesn't have a ballpoint pen or even a pencil in his pocket, he has to keep the idea in his head until he can get to his quill and parchment.

He rushes back to his lodgings on Silver Street, ignoring the vendors hawking brooms, the coaches clattering by, the piteous wails of beggars and prisoners. Bounding up the stairs, he snatches his quill and starts to write furiously, not even bothering to light a candle against the dusk. "To be, or not to be," he scrawls, "that is the—." But the quill point has gone dull, the letters have fattened out illegibly, and in the middle of writing one of the most famous passages in the history of dramatic literature, Shakespeare has to stop to sharpen his pen.

Taking a deep breath, he lights a candle now that it's dark, sits down, and begins again. By the time the candle has burned out and the noisy apprentices of his French Huguenot landlord have quieted down, Shakespeare has finished Act 3 of *Hamlet* with scarcely a blot.

Early the next morning, he hurries through the fog of a London summer morning to the rooms of his colleague Richard Burbage, the actor for whom the role of Hamlet is being written. He finds Burbage asleep and snoring loudly, sprawled across his straw mattress. Not only had the actor performed in *Henry V* the previous afternoon, but he had then gone out carousing all night with some friends who had come to the performance.

Shakespeare shakes his friend awake, until, bleary-eyed, Burbage sits up in his bed. "Dammit, Will," he grumbles, "can't you let an honest man sleep?" But the playwright, his eyes shining and the words tumbling out of his mouth, says, "Shut up and listen—tell me what you think of *this*!"

He begins to read to the still half-asleep Burbage, pacing around the room as he speaks. ". . . Whether 'tis nobler in the mind to suffer the slings and arrows of outrageous fortune—"

Burbage interrupts, suddenly wide awake, "That's excellent, very good, 'the slings and arrows of outrageous fortune,' yes, I think it will work quite well. . . ." He takes the parchment from Shakespeare and murmurs the lines to himself, slowly at first but with growing excitement.

The sun is just coming up, and the words of one of Shakespeare's most famous soliloquies are being uttered for the first time by the first actor ever to bring Hamlet to life. It must have been an exhilarating moment.

Shakespeare wrote most of his plays to be performed live by the actor Richard Burbage and the rest of the Lord Chamberlain's men (later the King's men). Today, however, our first encounter with the plays is usually in the form of the printed word. And there is no question that reading Shakespeare for the first time isn't easy. His plays aren't comic books or magazines or the dime-store detective novels I read when I was young. A lot of his sentences are complex. Many of his words are no longer used in our everyday

speech. His profound thoughts are often condensed into poetry, which is not as straightforward as prose.

Yet when you hear the words spoken aloud, a lot of the
language may strike you as unexpectedly modern. For
Shakespeare's plays, like any dramatic work, weren't really
meant to be read; they were meant to be spoken, seen, and
performed. It's amazing how lines that are so troublesome
in print can flow so naturally and easily when spoken.

I think it was precisely this music that first fascinated
me. When I was growing up, Shakespeare was a stranger to
me. I had no particular interest in him, for I was from a
different cultural tradition. It never occurred to me that his
plays might be more than just something to "get through"
in school, like science or math or the physical education
requirement we had to fulfill. My passions then were
movies, radio, and vaudeville—certainly not Elizabethan
drama.

I was, however, fascinated by words and language. Because I grew up in a home where Yiddish was spoken, and
English was only a second language, I was acutely sensitive
to the musical sounds of different languages and had an ear
for lilt and cadence and rhythm in the spoken word. And so
I loved reciting poems and speeches even as a very young
child. In first grade I learned lots of short nature verses—
"Who has seen the wind?," one of them began. My first
foray into drama was playing the role of Scrooge in Charles
Dickens's *A Christmas Carol* when I was eight years old. I
liked summoning all the scorn and coldness I possessed
and putting them into the words, "Bah, humbug!"

From there I moved on to longer and more famous poems
and other works by writers of the 1930s. Then, in junior
high school, I made my first acquaintance with Shakespeare through his play *Julius Caesar*. Our teacher, Miss
McKay, assigned the class a passage to memorize from the
opening scene of the play, the one that begins "Wherefore
rejoice? What conquest brings he home?" The passage
seemed so wonderfully theatrical and alive to me, and the
experience of memorizing and reciting it was so much fun,
that I went on to memorize another speech from the play on
my own.

I chose Mark Antony's address to the crowd in Act 3,

scene 2, which struck me then as incredibly high drama.
Even today, when I speak the words, I feel the same thrill I
did that first time. There is the strong and athletic Antony
descending from the raised pulpit where he has been speaking, right into the midst of a crowded Roman square. Hold-
ing the torn and bloody cloak of the murdered Julius
Caesar in his hand, he begins to speak to the people of
Rome:

> If you have tears, prepare to shed them now.
> You all do know this mantle. I remember
> The first time ever Caesar put it on;
> 'Twas on a summer's evening in his tent,
> That day he overcame the Nervii.
> Look, in this place ran Cassius' dagger through.
> See what a rent the envious Casca made.
> Through this the well-belovèd Brutus stabbed,
> And as he plucked his cursèd steel away,
> Mark how the blood of Caesar followed it,
> As rushing out of doors to be resolved
> If Brutus so unkindly knocked or no;
> For Brutus, as you know, was Caesar's angel.
> Judge, O you gods, how dearly Caesar loved him!
> This was the most unkindest cut of all . . .

I'm not sure now that I even knew Shakespeare had written a lot of other plays, or that he was considered "time-
less," "universal," or "classic"—but I knew a good speech
when I heard one, and I found the splendid rhythms of
Antony's rhetoric as exciting as anything I'd ever come
across.

Fifty years later, I still feel that way. Hearing good actors
speak Shakespeare gracefully and naturally is a wonderful
experience, unlike any other I know. There's a satisfying
fullness to the spoken word that the printed page just can't
convey. This is why seeing the plays of Shakespeare performed live in a theater is the best way to appreciate them.
If you can't do that, listening to sound recordings or watching film versions of the plays is the next best thing.

But if you do start with the printed word, use the play as a
script. Be an actor yourself and say the lines out loud. Don't
worry too much at first about words you don't immediately
understand. Look them up in the footnotes or a dictionary,

but don't spend too much time on this. It is more profitable (and fun) to get the sense of a passage and sing it out. Speak naturally, almost as if you were talking to a friend, but be sure to enunciate the words properly. You'll be surprised at how much you understand simply by speaking the speech "trippingly on the tongue," as Hamlet advises the Players.

You might start, as I once did, with a speech from *Julius Caesar*, in which the tribune (city official) Marullus scolds the commoners for transferring their loyalties so quickly from the defeated and murdered general Pompey to the newly victorious Julius Caesar:

> Wherefore rejoice? What conquest brings he home?
> What tributaries follow him to Rome
> To grace in captive bonds his chariot wheels?
> You blocks, you stones, you worse than senseless things!
> O you hard hearts, you cruel men of Rome,
> Knew you not Pompey? Many a time and oft
> Have you climbed up to walls and battlements,
> To towers and windows, yea, to chimney tops,
> Your infants in your arms, and there have sat
> The livelong day, with patient expectation,
> To see great Pompey pass the streets of Rome.

With the exception of one or two words like "wherefore" (which means "why," not "where"), "tributaries" (which means "captives"), and "patient expectation" (which means patient waiting), the meaning and emotions of this speech can be easily understood.

From here you can go on to dialogues or other more challenging scenes. Although you may stumble over unaccustomed phrases or unfamiliar words at first, and even fall flat when you're crossing some particularly rocky passages, pick yourself up and stay with it. Remember that it takes time to feel at home with anything new. Soon you'll come to recognize Shakespeare's unique sense of humor and way of saying things as easily as you recognize a friend's laughter.

And then it will just be a matter of choosing which one of Shakespeare's plays you want to tackle next. As a true fan of his, you'll find that you're constantly learning from his plays. It's a journey of discovery that you can continue for the rest of your life. For no matter how many times you read or see a particular play, there will always be something new there that you won't have noticed before.

Why do so many thousands of people get hooked on Shakespeare and develop a habit that lasts a lifetime? What can he really say to us today, in a world filled with inventions and problems he never could have imagined? And how do you get past his special language and difficult sentence structure to understand him?

The best way to answer these questions is to go see a live production. You might not know much about Shakespeare, or much about the theater, but when you watch actors performing one of his plays on the stage, it will soon become clear to you why people get so excited about a playwright who lived hundreds of years ago.

For the story—what's happening in the play—is the most accessible part of Shakespeare. In *A Midsummer Night's Dream*, for example, you can immediately understand the situation: a girl is chasing a guy who's chasing a girl who's chasing another guy. No wonder *A Midsummer Night's Dream* is one of the most popular of Shakespeare's plays: it's about one of the world's most popular pastimes—falling in love.

But the course of true love never did run smooth, as the young suitor Lysander says. Often in Shakespeare's comedies the girl whom the guy loves doesn't love him back, or she loves him but he loves someone else. In *The Two Gentlemen of Verona*, Julia loves Proteus, Proteus loves Sylvia, and Sylvia loves Valentine, who is Proteus's best friend. In the end, of course, true love prevails, but not without lots of complications along the way.

For in all of his plays—comedies, histories, and tragedies—Shakespeare is showing you human nature. His characters act and react in the most extraordinary ways—and sometimes in the most incomprehensible ways. People are always trying to find motivations for what a character does. They ask, "Why does Iago want to destroy Othello?"

The answer, to me, is very simple—because that's the way Iago is. That's just his nature. Shakespeare doesn't explain his characters; he sets them in motion—and away they go. He doesn't worry about whether they're likable or not. He's interested in interesting people, and his most fascinating characters are those who are unpredictable. If you lean back in your chair early on in one of his plays, thinking you've figured out what Iago or Shylock (in *The Merchant of Venice*) is up to, don't be too sure—because that great judge of human nature, Shakespeare, will surprise you every time.

He is just as wily in the way he structures a play. In *Macbeth*, a comic scene is suddenly introduced just after the bloodiest and most treacherous slaughter imaginable, of a guest and king by his host and subject, when in comes a drunk porter who has to go to the bathroom. Shakespeare is tickling your emotions by bringing a stand-up comic on-stage right on the heels of a savage murder.

It has taken me thirty years to understand even some of these things, and so I'm not suggesting that Shakespeare is immediately understandable. I've gotten to know him not through theory but through practice, the practice of the *living* Shakespeare—the playwright of the theater.

Of course the plays are a great achievement of dramatic literature, and they should be studied and analyzed in schools and universities. But you must always remember, when reading all the words *about* the playwright and his plays, that *Shakespeare's* words came first and that in the end there is nothing greater than a single actor on the stage speaking the lines of Shakespeare.

Everything important that I know about Shakespeare comes from the practical business of producing and directing his plays in the theater. The task of classifying, criticizing, and editing Shakespeare's printed works I happily leave to others. For me, his plays really do live on the stage, not on the page. That is what he wrote them for and that is how they are best appreciated.

Although Shakespeare lived and wrote hundreds of years ago, his name rolls off my tongue as if he were my brother. As a producer and director, I feel that there is a professional relationship between us that spans the centuries. As a human being, I feel that Shakespeare has enriched my understanding of life immeasurably. I hope you'll let him do the same for you.

❖

People always say that *Macbeth* is a play about ambition. But ambition is too vague a word to describe what goes on in the minds of Macbeth and Lady Macbeth. Their ambition is a dark driving force that will never be satisfied by what it achieves. It's an ambition that relies purely on getting other people out of the way, an ambition that requires one murder after another until Macbeth is "in blood / Stepped in so far that, should I wade no more, / Returning were as tedious as go o'er." The kind of ambition that Macbeth and his wife have feeds on itself, growing steadily and inevitably until it finally comes to rest with their deaths.

Though it is a tragedy, *Macbeth* is preoccupied with the perpetuation of the royal bloodline, as are many of Shakespeare's history plays. This concern seems to be at the core of Macbeth's ambition. His own quest, strangely resembling Richard III's, focuses on eliminating whoever is in the way of his becoming king.

And so he starts with the murder of King Duncan, the hereditary monarch. But it's clear to the murdered king's sons, Malcolm and Donalbain, that they are the next targets, and so they immediately flee Macbeth's castle. Then, in order to thwart the prophecy that Banquo will be father to a line of kings, Macbeth arranges to have him and his heir, Fleance, killed. When he learns to his horror that Fleance, like Malcolm and Donalbain, has escaped, he grows frantic at the failure of his efforts to achieve his bloody goal.

With an unquenchable appetite for murder, he orders the slaughter of Macduff's wife, children, and servants. The scene where Macduff learns of this butchery by Macbeth's henchmen is tremendously moving. Is there any greater expression of human grief than these lines spoken by the stricken Macduff?

> He has no children. All my pretty ones?
> Did you say all? O hell-kite! All?
> What, all my pretty chickens and their dam
> At one fell swoop?

The adolescent Malcolm, who has little experience in human affairs, appeals to his maleness, saying, "Dispute it like a man." Macduff's quiet reply, which always moves me deeply, is: "I shall do so; / But I must also feel it as a man." This is beautiful writing.

Gray, misty, and dark, *Macbeth* is a play in charcoal, with splotches of red providing the only color. Shakespeare, always attentive to his audience, gives them the revenge they want—everyone is eager to see Macbeth get it at the end, and he does. But Shakespeare doesn't satisfy the crowd's bloodlust right away. Macbeth is given his day in court, too, as he invites all comers into the fray: "Blow wind, come wrack, / At least we'll die with harness on our back."

Obviously Shakespeare doesn't resort to simplistic stereotypes. He lets good and bad mingle within Macbeth's heart—and within the hearts of all his bloody villains, for that matter. Richard III, that villain-king par excellence, fights to the bitter end, uttering those immortal lines. "A horse! A horse! My kingdom for a horse!" And Iago, the consummate evildoer, retains a shred of self-possession—even self-respect—at the end of *Othello* when he says, "Demand me nothing. What you know, you know. / From this time forth I never will speak word." With Iago, as with Richard and Macbeth, Shakespeare reminds us that people are never as simple as they seem.

JOSEPH PAPP

JOSEPH PAPP GRATEFULLY ACKNOWLEDGES THE HELP OF ELIZABETH KIRKLAND IN PREPARING THIS FOREWORD.

MACBETH

Introduction

Macbeth is seemingly the last of four great Shakespearean tragedies—*Hamlet* (c. 1599–1601), *Othello* (c. 1603–1604), *King Lear* (c. 1605), and *Macbeth* (c. 1606–1607)—that examine the dimensions of spiritual evil, as distinguished from the political strife of Roman tragedies such as *Julius Caesar*, *Antony and Cleopatra*, and *Coriolanus*. Whether or not Shakespeare intended *Macbeth* as a culmination of a series of tragedies on evil, the play does offer a particularly terse and gloomy view of humanity's encounter with the powers of darkness. Macbeth, more consciously than any other of Shakespeare's major tragic protagonists, has to face the temptation of committing what he knows to be a monstrous crime. Like Doctor Faustus in Christopher Marlowe's play *The Tragedy of Doctor Faustus* (c. 1588–1592), and to a lesser extent like Adam in John Milton's *Paradise Lost* (1667), Macbeth understands the reasons for resisting evil and yet goes ahead with his disastrous plan. His awareness of and sensitivity to moral issues, together with his conscious choice of evil, produce an unnerving account of human failure, all the more distressing because Macbeth is so representatively human. He seems to possess freedom of will and accepts personal responsibility for his fate, and yet his tragic doom seems unavoidable. Nor is there eventual salvation to be hoped for, as there is in *Paradise Lost*, since Macbeth's crime is too heinous and his heart too hardened. He is more like Doctor Faustus, damned and in despair.

To an extent not found in the other tragedies, the issue is stated in terms of salvation versus damnation. Macbeth knows before he acts that Duncan's virtues "Will plead like angels, trumpet-tongued, against / The deep damnation of his taking-off" (1.7.19–20). After the murder, he is equally aware that he has "Put rancors in the vessel of my peace . . . and mine eternal jewel / Given to the common enemy of man" (3.1.68–70). His enemies later describe him as a devil and a "hellhound" (5.8.3). He, like Marlowe's Doctor Faustus before him, has knowingly sold his soul for gain. And although as a mortal he still has time to repent his crimes, horrible as they are, Macbeth cannot find the words to be penitent. "Wherefore could not I pronounce 'Amen'?" he implores his wife after they have committed the murder. "I had most need of blessing, and 'Amen' / Stuck in my throat" (2.2.35–37). Macbeth's own answer seems to be that he has committed himself so inexorably to evil that he cannot turn back. Sentence has been pronounced: "Glamis hath murdered sleep, and therefore Cawdor / Shall sleep no more; Macbeth shall sleep no more" (ll. 46–47).

Macbeth is not a conventional morality play (even less so than *Doctor Faustus*) and is not concerned primarily with preaching against sinfulness or demonstrating that Macbeth is finally damned for what he does. A tradition of moral and religious drama has been transformed into an intensely human study of the psychological effects of evil on a particular man and, to a lesser extent, on his wife. That moral tradition nevertheless provides as its legacy a perspective on the operation of evil in human affairs. A perverse ambition seemingly inborn in Macbeth himself is abetted by dark forces dwelling in the universe, waiting to catch him off guard. Among Shakespeare's tragedies, indeed, *Macbeth* is remarkable for its focus on evil in the protagonist, and on his relationship to the sinister forces tempting him. In no other Shakespearean play do we identify to such an extent with the evildoer himself. *Richard III* also focuses on an evil protagonist, but in that play we are distanced by the character's gloating and are not partakers in the introspective soliloquies of a man confronting his own ambition. Macbeth is more like us. We share Macbeth's inclination toward brutality, as well as his humane resistance of that urge. We witness and struggle to understand his downfall through two phases: the spiritual struggle before he actually commits the crime, and the despairing aftermath with its vain quest for security through continued violence. Evil is thus presented in two aspects, first as insidious suggestion leading us on toward an illusory promise of gain, and then as frenzied addiction to the hated thing by which we are possessed.

In the first phase, before the commission of the crime, we wonder to what extent the powers of darkness are a determining factor in what Macbeth does. Can he avoid the fate the witches proclaim? Evidently he and Lady Macbeth have previously considered murdering Duncan; the witches appear after the thought, not before. Lady Macbeth reminds her wavering husband that he was the first to "break this enterprise" to her, on some previous occasion when "Nor time nor place / Did then adhere, and yet you would make both" (1.7.49–53). Elizabethans would understand that evil spirits such as witches appear when summoned, whether by our conscious or unconscious minds. Macbeth is ripe for their insinuations. A mind free of taint would see no sinister invitation in their prophecy of greatness to come. And in a saner moment Macbeth knows that his restless desire to interfere with destiny is arrogant and useless. "If chance will have me king, why, chance may crown me / Without my stir" (1.3.145–146). Banquo, his companion, serves as his dramatic opposite by consistently displaying the correct attitude toward the witches. "Speak then to me," he addresses them, "who neither beg nor fear / Your favors nor your hate" (ll. 60–61). Like Horatio in *Hamlet*, Banquo strongly resists the blandishments of fortune as well as its buffets, though not without an agonizing night of moral struggle. Indeed, promises of success are often more ruinous than setbacks—as in the seemingly paradoxical instance of the farmer, cited by Macbeth's porter, who "hanged himself on th' expectation of plenty" (2.3.4–5). It is by showing Macbeth that he is two-thirds of his way to the throne that the witches tempt him to seize the last third at whatever cost. "Glamis, and Thane of Cawdor! / The greatest is behind"(1.3.116–117).

Banquo comprehends the nature of temptation. "To win us to our harm," he observes, "The instruments of darkness tell us truths, / Win us with honest trifles, to betray 's / In deepest consequence" (1.3.123–126). The devil can speak true, and his strategy is to invite us into a trap we help prepare. Without our active consent in evil (as Othello also learns) we cannot fall. Yet in what sense are the witches trifling with Macbeth, or prevaricating? When they address him as one "that shalt be king hereafter" (l. 50), they are stating a certainty, for they can "look into the seeds of time / And say which grain will grow and which will not," as Banquo says (ll. 58–59). They know that Banquo will be "Lesser than Macbeth, and greater, / Not so happy, yet much happier" (ll. 65–66), since Banquo will beget a race of kings and Macbeth will not. How then do they know that

Macbeth will be king? If we consider the hypothetical question, what if Macbeth does *not* murder Duncan, we can gain some understanding of the relationship between character and fate; for the only valid answer is that the question remains hypothetical, Macbeth *does* kill Duncan, the witches are right in their prediction. It is idle to speculate that providence would have found another way to make Macbeth king, for the witches' prophecy is self-fulfilling in the very way they foresee. Character is fate; they know Macbeth's fatal weakness and know they can "enkindle" him to seize the crown by laying irresistible temptations before him. This does not mean that they determine his choice, but rather that Macbeth's choice is predictable and therefore unavoidable, even though not preordained. He has free choice, but that choice will in fact go only one way—as with Adam and Eve in Milton's *Paradise Lost* and in the medieval tradition from which this poem was derived.

Although the powers of evil cannot determine Macbeth's choice, they can influence the external conditions affecting that choice. By a series of apparently circumstantial events, well timed in their effect, they can repeatedly assail him just when he is about to rally to the call of conscience. The witches, armed with supernatural knowledge, inform Macbeth of his new title shortly before the King's ambassadors confirm that he is to be the Thane of Cawdor. Duncan chooses this night to lodge under Macbeth's roof. And just when Macbeth resolves to abandon even this unparalleled opportunity, his wife intervenes on the side of the witches. Macbeth commits the murder in part to keep his word to her and to prove he is no coward (like Donwald, the slayer of King Duff in one of Shakespeare's chief sources, Raphael Holinshed's *Chronicles*). Not only the opportunities presented to Macbeth but the obstacles put in his way are cannily timed to overwhelm his conscience. When King Duncan announces that his son Malcolm is now Prince of Cumberland and official heir to the throne (1.4), the unintended threat deflects Macbeth's mood from one of gratitude and acceptance to one of hostility. These are mitigating circumstances that affect our judgment of Macbeth, and even though they cannot excuse him they certainly increase our sympathetic identification.

We are moved too by the poetic intensity of Macbeth's

moral vision. His soliloquies are memorable as poetry, not merely because Shakespeare wrote them, but because Macbeth is sensitive and aware. The horror, indeed, of his crime is that his cultivated self is revolted by what he cannot prevent himself from doing. He understands with a terrible clarity not only the moral wrong of what he is about to do, but also the inescapably destructive consequences for himself. He is as reluctant as we to see the crime committed, and yet he goes to it with a sad and rational deliberateness rather than in a self-blinding fury. For Macbeth there is no seeming loss of perspective, and yet there is total alienation of the act from his moral consciousness. The arguments for and against murdering Duncan, as Macbeth pictures them in his acutely visual imagination, when weighed are overwhelmingly opposed to the deed. Duncan is his king and his guest, deserving Macbeth's duty and hospitality. The King is virtuous and able. He has shown every favor to Macbeth, thereby removing any sane motive for striving after further promotion. All human history shows that murders of this sort "return / To plague th' inventor" (1.7.9–10)—that is, provide only guilt and punishment rather than satisfaction. Finally, judgment in "the life to come" includes the prospect of eternal torment. On the other side of the argument is nothing but Macbeth's "Vaulting ambition, which o'erleaps itself" (l. 27)—a perverse refusal to be content with his present good fortune because there is more that beckons. Who could weigh the issues so dispassionately and still choose the wrong? The answer apparently is that we all could, for Macbeth strikes us as typically human both in his understanding and in his perverse ambition.

Macbeth's clarity of moral imagination is contrasted with his wife's imperceptiveness. He is always seeing visions or hearing voices—a dagger in the air, the ghost of Banquo, a voice crying "Sleep no more!"—and she is always denying them. "The sleeping and the dead / Are but as pictures," she insists. He knows that "all great Neptune's ocean" cannot wash the blood from his hands; "No, this my hand will rather / The multitudinous seas incarnadine, / Making the green one red." To Lady Macbeth, contrastingly, "A little water clears us of this deed. / How easy is it, then!" (2.2.57–72). Macbeth knows that the murder of Duncan is but the beginning: "We have scorched the snake, not killed it." Lady Macbeth would prefer to believe that "What's done is done" (3.2.14–15). Ironically, it is she finally who must endure visions of the most agonizing sort, sleepwalking in her madness and trying to rub away the "damned spot" that before seemed so easy to remove. "All the perfumes of Arabia will not sweeten this little hand," she laments (5.1.34–51). This relationship between Macbeth and Lady Macbeth owes much to traditional contrasts between male and female principles. As in the pairing of Adam and Eve, the man is the more rational of the two but knowingly shares his wife's sin through fondness for her. She has failed to foresee the long-range consequences of sinful ambition and so becomes a temptress to her husband. The fall of man takes place in an incongruous atmosphere of domestic intimacy and mutual concern; Lady Macbeth is motivated by ambition for her husband in much the same way that he sins to win her approbation.

The fatal disharmony flawing this domestic accord is conveyed through images of sexual inversion. Lady Macbeth prepares for her ordeal with the incantation, "Come, you spirits / That tend on mortal thoughts, unsex me here . . . Come to my woman's breasts / And take my milk for gall" (1.5.40–48). When she accuses her husband of unmanly cowardice and vows she would dash out the brains of her own infant for such effeminacy as he has displayed, he extols her with "Bring forth men-children only! / For thy undaunted mettle should compose / Nothing but males" (1.7.73–75). She takes the initiative, devising and then carrying out the plan to drug Duncan's chamber-guards with wine. This assumption of the dominant male role by the woman would again bring to the Elizabethan mind numerous biblical, medieval, and classical parallels deploring the ascendancy of passion over reason: Eve choosing for Adam, Noah's wife taking command of the ark, the Wife of Bath dominating her husbands, Venus emasculating Mars, and others.

In *Macbeth* sexual inversion also allies Lady Macbeth with the witches or weird sisters, the bearded women. Their unnaturalness betokens disorder in nature, for they can sail in a sieve and "look not like th' inhabitants o' th' earth / And yet are on 't" (1.3.41–42). Characteristically they speak in paradoxes: "When the battle's lost and won,"

"Fair is foul, and foul is fair" (1.1.4,11). Shakespeare probably drew on numerous sources to depict the witches: Holinshed's *Chronicles* (in which he conflated two accounts,
one of Duncan and Macbeth, and the other of King Duff
slain by Donwald with the help of his wife), King James's
writings on witchcraft, Samuel Harsnett's *Declaration of
Egregious Popish Impostures* (used also for *King Lear*), and
the accounts of the Scottish witch trials published around
1590. In the last, particularly, Shakespeare could have
found mention of witches raising storms and sailing in
sieves to endanger vessels at sea, performing threefold rit-
uals blaspheming the Trinity, and brewing witches' broth.
Holinshed's *Chronicles* refer to the weird sisters as "goddesses of destiny," associating them with the three fates,
Clotho, Lachesis, and Atropos, who spin, pull, and cut the
thread of life. In *Macbeth* the weird sisters' power to control fortune is curtailed, and they are portrayed as witches
according to popular contemporary understanding rather
than as goddesses of destiny; nonetheless, witches were
thought to be servants of the devil (Banquo wonders if the
devil can speak true in their utterances, 1.3.107), and
through them Macbeth has made an ominous pact with evil
itself. His visit to their seething cauldron in Act 4, scene 1,
brings him to the witches' masters, those unknown powers
that know his very thought and who tempt him with those
equivocations of which Banquo has warned Macbeth. The
popularity of witchlore tempted Shakespeare's acting company to expand the witches' scenes with spectacles of song
and dance; even the Folio text we have evidently contains
interpolations derived in part from Thomas Middleton's
The Witch (see especially 3.5 and part of 4.1 containing
mention of Middleton's songs "Come away" and "Black
spirits"). Nevertheless, Shakespeare's original theme of a
disharmony in nature remains clearly visible.

Patterns of imagery throughout the play point to the
same disorder in nature and in man. The murder of Duncan, like that of Caesar in *Julius Caesar,* is accompanied by
signs of the heavens' anger. Various observers report that
chimneys blow down during the unruly night, that owls
clamor and attack falcons, that the earth shakes, and that
Duncan's horses devour each other. (Some of these portents
are from Holinshed.) Banquo's ghost returns from the dead

to haunt his murderer, prompting Macbeth to speak in metaphors of charnel houses and graves that send back their dead and of birds of prey that devour the corpses. The drunken porter who opens the gate to Macduff and Lennox after the murder (2.3) invokes images of judgment and everlasting bonfire through which the scene takes on the semblance of hell gate and the Harrowing of Hell. Owls appear repeatedly in the imagery, along with other creatures associated with nighttime and horror: wolves, serpents, scorpions, bats, toads, beetles, crows, rooks. Darkness itself assumes tangible and menacing shapes of hidden stars or extinguished candles, a thick blanket shrouded "in the dunnest smoke of hell" (1.5.51), an entombment of the earth in place of "living light" (2.4.10), a scarf to hoodwink the eye of "pitiful day" (3.2.50), and a bloody and invisible hand to tear to pieces the lives of virtuous men. Sleep is transformed from "great nature's second course" and a "nourisher" of life that "knits up the raveled sleave of care" (2.2.41–44) into "death's counterfeit" (2.3.77) and a living hell for Lady Macbeth. Life becomes sterile for Macbeth, a denial of harvest, the lees or dregs of the wine and "the sere, the yellow leaf" (5.3.23). In a theatrical metaphor life becomes for him unreal, "a walking shadow, a poor player / That struts and frets his hour upon the stage / And then is heard no more" (5.5.24–26). This theme of empty illusion carries over into the recurring image of borrowed or ill-fitting garments that belie the wearer. Macbeth is an actor, a hypocrite, whose "False face must hide what the false heart doth know" (1.7.83) and who must "Look like th' innocent flower, / But be the serpent under 't" (1.5.65–66). Even the show of grief is an assumed mask whereby evildoers deceive the virtuous, so much so that Malcolm, Donalbain, and Macduff learn to conceal their true feeling rather than be thought to "show an unfelt sorrow" (2.3.138).

Blood is not only a literal sign of disorder but an emblem of Macbeth's remorseless butchery, a "damned spot" on the conscience, and a promise of divine vengeance: "It will have blood, they say; blood will have blood" (3.4.123). The emphasis on corrupted blood also suggests disease, in which Macbeth's tyranny is a sickness to his country as well as to himself. Scotland bleeds (4.3.32), needing a physician; Macduff and his allies call themselves "the medicine of the sickly weal" (5.2.27). Lady Macbeth's disease is incurable, something spiritually corrupt wherein "the patient / Must minister to himself" (5.3.47–48). Conversely, the English King Edward is renowned for his divine gift of curing what was called the king's evil, or scrofula.

Throughout, the defenders of righteousness are associated with positive images of natural order. Duncan rewards his subjects by saying, "I have begun to plant thee, and will labor / To make thee full of growing" (1.4.28–29). His arrival at Inverness Castle is heralded by signs of summer, sweet air, and "the temple-haunting martlet" (1.6.4). He is a fatherly figure, so much so that even Lady Macbeth balks at an act so like patricide. Macduff too is a father and husband whose family is butchered. The forest of Birnam marching to confront Macbeth, although rationally explainable as a device of camouflage for Macduff's army, is emblematic of the natural order itself rising up against the monstrosity of Macbeth's crimes. Banquo is above all a patriarchal figure, ancestor of the royal line governing Scotland and England at the time the play was written. These harmonies are to an extent restorative. Even the witches' riddling prophecies, "th' equivocation of the fiend" (5.5.43) luring Macbeth into further atrocities with the vain promise of security, anticipate a just retribution.

Nonetheless, the play's vision of evil shakes us deeply. Scotland's peace has been violated, so much so that "to do harm / Is often laudable, to do good sometimes / Accounted dangerous folly" (4.2.76–78). Lady Macduff and her son, along with young Siward, have had to pay with their innocent lives the terrible price of Scotland's tyranny; in his frenzied attempt to prevent the fulfillment of the prophecy about Banquo's lineage inheriting the kingdom, Macbeth has, like King Herod, slaughtered much of the younger generation on whom the future depends. We can only hope that the stability to which Scotland returns after his death will be lasting. Banquo's line is to rule eventually and to produce a line of kings reaching down to the royal occupant to whom Shakespeare will present his play, but when *Macbeth* ends, it is Malcolm who is king. The killing of a traitor (Macbeth) and the placing of his head on a pole replicate the play's beginning in the treason and beheading of the Thane of Cawdor—a gentleman on whom Duncan built "An absolute trust" (1.4.14). Most troublingly, the humanly representative nature of Macbeth's crime leaves us with little assurance that we could resist his temptation. The most that can be said is that wise and good men such as Banquo and Macduff have learned to know the evil in themselves and to resist it as nobly as they can.

Macbeth
in Performance

Theater managers have too often been unwilling to leave *Macbeth* as Shakespeare wrote it. The tampering began even during Shakespeare's lifetime or shortly thereafter. Added music and business for the witches must have been included in performances prior to 1623, since interpolations of this sort are found in the original Folio text published in that year. Act 3, scene 5, consisting chiefly of an unnecessary appearance by the witch Hecate, is probably by another author, and the song "Black Spirits" in Act 4, scene 1, is from a play by Thomas Middleton.

To be sure, Simon Forman's description of his visit to the Globe Theatre on April 20, 1611, suggests that he saw something close to what Shakespeare wrote. Forman, an astrologer and quack doctor, tells of Macbeth and Banquo "riding through a wood" (were Richard Burbage and a fellow actor on horseback?) where they encountered "three women fairies or nymphs" who saluted Macbeth, "saying three times to him, 'Hail, Macbeth, King of Codon'" (i.e., Thane of Cawdor). Forman goes on to describe a banquet at which Macbeth "began to speak of noble Banquo, and to wish that he were there. And as he thus did, standing up to drink a carouse to him, the ghost of Banquo came and sat down in his chair beside him. And he, turning about to sit down again, saw the ghost of Banquo, which fronted [affronted] him so that he fell into a great passion of fear and fury." All this sounds close to Shakespeare's text, as one would expect of a performance some three or four years after Shakespeare wrote the play and while he was still an active member of his acting company, the King's men. *Macbeth* probably remained in repertory during those years. Richard Burbage is likely to have played Macbeth, and John Rice, a boy actor in the company, may have played Lady Macbeth in 1611 when Forman saw the play. But fidelity to Shakespeare's intention was not to continue for long.

The play that diarist Samuel Pepys saw and enjoyed in the 1660s had already been expanded to include a good deal of new spectacle. Pepys marveled, on April 19, 1667: "Here we saw *Macbeth*, which, though I have seen it often, yet it is one of the best plays for a stage, and variety of dancing and music, that ever I saw." Earlier, in January of the same year, Pepys especially liked the "divertissement," that is to say the song and dance. William Davenant provided the altered and augmented script for this production, not only amplifying the original through operatic and scenic splendor, but also symmetrically balancing the play with an enlarged role for Lady Macduff so that her invincible virtue might offset the wickedness of Lady Macbeth. A production of Davenant's version in 1672 at the Dorset Garden Theatre, according to John Downes, showed the play "being dressed in all its finery, as new clothes, new scenes, machines, as flyings for the witches, with all the swinging and dancing in it." Music was provided by Matthew Locke and others. Thomas Betterton enjoyed one of his great successes as Macbeth, and continued to play the part until 1707. The witches flew, danced, sang, and otherwise amused the spectators; their parts were taken by comic actors, and their costumes were meant to invite laughter.

Macbeth had become something of an opera. The scenic effects and additional stage business were simply irresistible, and audiences continued to demand more than Shakespeare had provided. The operatic tradition continued well into the eighteenth century after Betterton had been succeeded as Macbeth by John Mills and James Quin, and Mary Porter had emerged as the most remarkable Lady Macbeth of the era—even better than Hannah Pritchard, according to the actor Charles Macklin.

David Garrick made an attempt to restore Shakespeare's play in 1744, though at the last minute, afraid of an adverse reaction, he partly backed down. He did reintroduce some of Shakespeare's language, permitted the witches to rise from under the stage rather than enter in flight, and cut away the platitudinous moralisms that Davenant had supplied for Lady Macduff. On the other hand he omitted the murder of Lady Macduff and her son (4.2), left out the drunken Porter (2.3) as a blatant violation of classical strictures against including comic material in a tragedy, and then, somewhat incongruously perhaps, continued to provide the diverting song and dance of the witches to which audiences had grown so accustomed. Despite these unreformed accretions, Garrick's interpretation of the lead role contributed to a new understanding of Shakespeare's artistry. Garrick's thoughtful soliloquies, intimately shared with the audience in the small Theatre Royal, Drury Lane, presented Macbeth as a sensitive and poetic man caught up in the horrid deed he could not resist. Hannah Pritchard, physically towering over Garrick as Lady Macbeth, was, in Thomas Davies's words, "insensible to compunction and inflexibly bent to cruelty" as she shamed Macbeth into action with her ferocious strength of spirit. Together, this famous pair performed so compellingly that they lent authority and impetus to the new movement in literary criticism toward the study of character as the central feature of Shakespearean drama.

Garrick performed *Macbeth* in contemporary eighteenth-century dress. The movement toward naturalistic and authentic setting and costume, with which the nineteenth century was to be increasingly fascinated, seems to have begun with West Digges at Edinburgh in 1757 and then Charles Macklin at Covent Garden in 1773, both of whom dressed in historical Scottish garb. (Garrick considered the idea in 1772 but finally rejected it.) Macklin's costumes and sets were as yet far from accurate—he included cannon for Macbeth's castle in a presumably eleventh-century Scottish setting long before the discovery of gunpowder, dressed Lady Macbeth in modern robes, and indeed wore a tunic himself that reflected early sixteenth- rather than eleventh-century fashion—but his attempt at least attested to a growing interest in historical realism.

John Philip Kemble's production at Drury Lane in 1794 was, according to theater historian and producer W. C. Oulton, distinguished by its realistic attention to the appearance of the witches: they were no longer dressed in "mittens, plaited caps, laced aprons, red stomachers, ruffs, etc., which was the dress of those weird sisters when Mesdames Beard, Champness, etc. represented them with Garrick's *Macbeth*," but appeared as "preternatural beings, distinguished only by the fellness of their purposes and the fatality of their delusions." In the cauldron scene, serpents writhed around the evil spirits. Kemble was the first to treat Banquo's ghost as a phantasm seen only by Macbeth.

Kemble's famous leading lady (and sister), Sarah Siddons, offered an intensely psychological portrayal of Lady Macbeth in the great tradition of Mary Porter and Hannah Pritchard. With her "turbulent and inhuman strength of spirit," so much admired by William Hazlitt, Siddons was also able, especially in the sleepwalking scene, to move audiences with the suggestion of a desolate and tortured soul. She and Kemble did much to further Garrick's and Pritchard's exploitation of character as the essence of Shakespearean tragedy, further humanizing the portraits that they had developed. Yet Kemble did little to take away Davenant's spectacle; Matthew Locke's music was still to be heard, and scenic extravagance was abetted by the large size of the Drury Lane theater after it was renovated in 1794 and by the capacity of the Theatre Royal, Covent Garden (where Kemble and Siddons performed in 1800, 1803, 1809, and afterward).

Still greater magnificence was on its way. Edmund Kean, a fierce devotee of visual authenticity, produced a version of *Macbeth* in 1814 that, along with the music of Locke, provided new scenery of a splendidly romantic cast: a rocky pass and a bridge, a gallery and banquet hall in Macbeth's castle, a cavern and "car of clouds," Hecate's cave, and much more. The ascent of Hecate in her chariot was particularly admired. Kean wore kilts over an armored breastplate in the first acts, as Kemble had done. William Charles Macready, who played Macbeth over a period of some thirty years (starting in 1820 at Covent Garden, and thereafter chiefly at Drury Lane opposite the brilliant Helen Faucit), devised striking atmospheric effects for his production at Drury Lane in 1837 in order to evoke the dark visionary realm that Macbeth inhabits. These effects included a mist that rose slowly in Act 1 to reveal a barren heath and highland landscape, a rustic bridge, later a royal march for Duncan, a castle interior at Dunsinane with torches and with servants carrying food, a walled courtyard of the same castle in Act 2, an opulent banquet scene, and a ghost entering through a trapdoor hidden from the audience by a cluster of servants. At Birnam Wood, each soldier was completely screened by the huge bough he carried, while the illusion of the forested army receded into the infinite distance of a diorama. To accommodate the scenic elaboration Macready could not play Shakespeare's complete text, omitting, among others, the Porter scene while preserving many of Davenant's hoary alterations.

Not until Samuel Phelps's production of 1847 at the Sadler's Wells Theatre, in fact, did a theater manager summon the resolution to do away with the witch scenes of Davenant and limit the music to between acts. Phelps went on to restore the Porter (though cutting the second half of his speech), the killing of Lady Macduff and her son onstage, and the killing of Macbeth offstage, as in Shakespeare's original. Objection was raised to the horror of some of Phelps's restorations, and in later productions he eliminated the murder of Macduff's young son and Macduff's entry with Macbeth's head on a pole. Phelps provided some striking effects of "darkness visible" by means of gauze screens and imaginative lighting. His own acting of Macbeth was rugged and energetic, less poetic and haunted than Macready's or Edwin Booth's, but, as one critic wrote, "robust and terrible, and, to my mind, closer to the spirit of Shakespeare."

Phelps's courageous restoration was almost immediately undone, however, by Charles Kean, who resuscitated Locke and Davenant in an especially magnificent spectacle at the Princess's Theatre in 1853. Gone once again was the scene of Lady Macduff and her son and the slaying of Macbeth offstage. Instead of striving for textual accuracy, Kean lavished all his attention on what he took to be an authentic reproduction of eleventh-century Scotland. Reasoning that the era in question was one of Danish invasion, Kean devised tunics, mantles, and cross-gartering of Danish and Anglo-Saxon style, along with feathered helmets, particolored woolens, and iron mail sewn on cloth or leather. His sets aimed at architectural reconstruction as well, with sloping roofs supported by Saxon pillars and the like. The Victorian age, besotted by the delights of scenic splendor in the theater, simply was not ready to give up the opportunities that Davenant and Locke had provided for visual and musical elaboration. Kean's production did not, to be sure, delight everyone: *Lloyd's Weekly* complained that "in Garrick's day we had a Macbeth without the costume, and now we have the costume without Macbeth." If the lavish spectacle, the inclusion of music, and the focus on the main characters at the expense of lesser figures threatened to overwhelm Shakespeare's play, it did provide the cultural matrix in which Giuseppe Verdi could write his Italian opera, *Macbeth* (first performed in 1847, revised in 1865).

Late nineteenth-century theater managers gave full expression to the prevailing taste in opulent historical realism. Henry Irving, at the Lyceum Theatre in 1875 and 1888, chose to revive eleventh-century Scotland once again while banishing Lady Macduff and her son and including songs from stage tradition, though he did restore the drunken Porter. Ellen Terry excelled in his 1888 production as Lady Macbeth: she was, as one critic wrote, "the stormy dominant woman of the eleventh century equipped with the capricious emotional subtlety of the nineteenth century." Sarah Bernhardt startled audiences in 1884 at the Gaiety Theatre by coming onstage in the sleepwalking scene barefoot and in a clinging nightdress. Tommaso Salvini (1884, Covent Garden) and Johnston Forbes-Robertson (1898, Lyceum Theatre) continued the tradition of bulky and nearly unmovable sets. Herbert Beerbohm Tree (1911, His Majesty's Theatre) paid particular attention to beautiful stage pictures—Lady Macbeth (Violet Vanbrugh) in a long scarf of crimson silk or veiled in black, Lady Macbeth ascending and descending a staircase in defiance of the requirements of Shakespeare's text for the sleepwalking scene, torches glowing in the dark, an exquisite set for the murder of Duncan—which inevitably required extensive cutting and reduction of the number of scenes. Frank Benson, who directed the play in nine different seasons between 1896 and 1911 at Stratford-upon-Avon, summed up in his own way what nineteenth-century staging and interpretation had to offer.

A new direction manifested itself in William Poel's return to the original Folio text in a performance by the Shakespeare Reading Society in 1895. Though anticipated by Garrick and especially Phelps in regard to textual restoration, Poel went beyond them in staging the play as an Elizabethan drama, not as a Scottish one, using Elizabethan dress and a thrust apron stage. Change was in the air, and by 1915 and 1918 Sybil Thorndike at the Old Vic played Lady Macbeth as though she and her husband were " 'big capitalists' in a tragic partnership" (Dennis Bartholomeusz, *Mac-*

beth and the Players, p. 226, quoting Thorndike). Lewis
Casson, at the Prince's Theatre in 1926, tried to reconcile
the scenic realism of Tree and Kean with Casson's interest
in the staging theories of Poel and Harley Granville-Barker.
Sybil Thorndike again played Lady Macbeth. Harcourt Wil-
liams, at the Old Vic in 1930, provided simple sets and
swift-paced action for John Gielgud's subtle portrait of
Macbeth's moral isolation. Tyrone Guthrie dropped the
witches from the opening scene of his Old Vic production of
1934, arguing that they should not be allowed to govern the
entire tragedy; his Macbeth, played by Charles Laughton
with Flora Robson as Lady Macbeth, was a man caught in
conflict between his noble qualities and the destructive ambition that those very qualities seemed to generate.

Innovation encouraged further experiment. Theodore
Komisarjevsky used modern dress against a backdrop of
the howitzers and field uniforms of World War I for his
Macbeth at Stratford-upon-Avon in 1933. Komisarjevsky's
witches were old hags who rifled the corpses of soldiers
slain in battle and used palmistry to tell the fortunes of
Macbeth and Banquo. John Gielgud directed Ralph Rich-
ardson as Macbeth at Stratford-upon-Avon in 1952 on an ab-
stract set of menacing dark masses lit only by torchlight. In
Glen Byam Shaw's memorable production at Stratford-
upon-Avon three years later, with Laurence Olivier and Vi-
vien Leigh as Macbeth and Lady Macbeth, the brutality of
the murder of Lady Macduff and her son was in keeping
with the production's bleakly formidable set and unspar-
ing confrontation with uncontrollable evil. Interpretations
have ranged from Guthrie's excision of the witches in Act 1,
scene 1, to more predetermined views of Macbeth's tragedy, as in Stratford, Ontario's *Macbeth* of 1983, in which the
witches hovered everywhere and even took the part of the
third murderer of Banquo so that they could enable
Fleance to escape as predicted, or the Kabuki *Macbeth* of
Chicago's Wisdom Bridge Theatre, 1983, in which the
witches were puppetmasters guiding the players in their
drama by invisible wires.

The twentieth century has been a time, then, of experi-
mentation in nonrepresentational staging and of candid ex-
ploration of evil in the context of modern experience with
war and terror. Orson Welles directed a *Macbeth* with an all

black cast at New York's Lafayette Theater in 1936, with the witches replaced by voodoo practitioners. Peter Hall's production at Stratford-upon-Avon in 1967 consciously explored what Hall termed "the metaphysics of evil," opening with a large white sheet that fluttered away at the approach of the witches to reveal a bloodred carpet. At Stratford, Ontario, in 1971, Peter Gill directed a *Macbeth* centered on the idea of tyranny, with throngs of "poor people" present as the silent victims of the powerful. In 1974, at the height of interest in the Watergate scandal, Edward Berkeley directed the play for the New York Shakespeare Festival, on a grim set composed of subway grates, as a study of public corruption and the inner wastage it involves. The following year, at Stratford-upon-Avon, Trevor Nunn produced a dark, brooding version of the play, with Nicol Williamson playing Macbeth, in the words of drama critic Irving Wardle, as "a secretive man who becomes more and more unreachable until by the end events are happening only in his head." Two years later, at The Other Place in Stratford, Nunn brilliantly directed Ian McKellen and Judi Dench on a small, bare stage with a few crates as props, emphasizing the claustrophobic world created by Macbeth's manic evil. Adrian Noble's *Macbeth*, starring Jonathan Pryce, at Stratford-upon-Avon in 1986, was domestic and introverted, all the more terrifying for being so, finding the tragedy in Macbeth's inability to live with the consequences of his actions and their ramifications. In whatever guise, and in spite of its notoriety for being bad luck in the theater, *Macbeth* has attracted a remarkable roster of great performers in recent years: Judith Anderson, Alec Guinness, Pamela Brown, Donald Wolfit, Michael Redgrave, Godfrey Tearle, Diana Wynyard, Paul Rogers, Albert Finney, Simone Signoret, Michael Hordern, Christopher Plummer, Eric Porter, Jason Robards, Jr., Christopher Walken, F. Murray Abraham, Janet Suzman, and Peter O'Toole, to name only some.

    Macbeth has also attracted the attention of gifted filmmakers. Orson Welles's *Macbeth* (1948), though marred by a low budget and some uneven acting, makes bold use of the film medium to support the psychological proposition that much of Macbeth's imagining is unreal. The camera is permitted to see—or not see—things from Macbeth's point of view by literally peering over his shoulder. Roman Polanski's *Macbeth* (1971) revels in the kind of graphic and sensational violence that film can exploit, establishing the deep pessimism of Polanski's vision. Macbeth's defeat does not signal a renewed order: Macduff's victory is achieved with a random blow, and the play ends with Donalbain now in search of the witches and his own crown. Beyond doubt the greatest film version of *Macbeth* is Akira Kurosawa's *Throne of Blood* (1957), in which the story of Macbeth is retold in terms of Japanese warlord history, with arresting images of mist-shrouded forests and mysteriously disappearing witches, and spare oriental interiors intensifying the loneliness of the murdering protagonists. Whenever it is performed, *Macbeth*'s desolating story of crime and tragic failure remains essentially timeless, even while it enables the performers to gather around them the particular forms of human gesture and experience through which succeeding generations of actors and playgoers have striven to understand Shakespeare's masterful play.

The Playhouse

This early copy of a drawing by Johannes de Witt of the Swan Theatre in London (c. 1596), made by his friend Arend van Buchell, is the only surviving contemporary sketch of the interior of a public theater in the 1590s.

From other contemporary evidence, including the stage directions and dialogue of Elizabethan plays, we can surmise that the various public theaters where Shakespeare's plays were produced (the Theatre, the Curtain, the Globe) resembled the Swan in many important particulars, though there must have been some variations as well. The public playhouses were essentially round, or polygonal, and open to the sky, forming an acting arena approximately 70 feet in diameter; they did not have a large curtain with which to open and close a scene, such as we see today in opera and some traditional theater. A platform measuring approximately 43 feet across and 27 feet deep, referred to in the de Witt drawing as the *proscaenium*, projected into the yard, *planities sive arena*. The roof, *tectum*, above the stage and supported by two pillars, could contain machinery for ascents and descents, as were required in several of Shakespeare's late plays. Above this roof was a hut, shown in the drawing with a flag flying atop it and a trumpeter at its door announcing the performance of a play. The underside of the stage roof, called the heavens, was usually richly decorated with symbolic figures of the sun, the moon, and the constellations. The platform stage stood at a height of $5\frac{1}{2}$ feet or so above the yard, providing room under the stage for underworldly effects. A trapdoor, which is not visible in this drawing, gave access to the space below.

The structure at the back of the platform (labeled *mimorum aedes*), known as the tiring-house because it was the actors' attiring (dressing) space, featured at least two doors, as shown here. Some theaters seem to have also had a discovery space, or curtained recessed alcove, perhaps between the two doors—in which Falstaff could have hidden from the sheriff (*1 Henry IV*, 2.4) or Polonius could have eavesdropped on Hamlet and his mother (*Hamlet*, 3.4). This discovery space probably gave the actors a means of access to and from the tiring-house. Curtains may also have been hung in front of the stage doors on occasion. The de Witt drawing shows a gallery above the doors that extends across the back and evidently contains spectators. On occasions when action "above" demanded the use of this space, as when Juliet appears at her "window" (*Romeo and Juliet*, 2.2 and 3.5), the gallery seems to have been used by the actors, but large scenes there were impractical.

The three-tiered auditorium is perhaps best described by Thomas Platter, a visitor to London in 1599 who saw on that occasion Shakespeare's *Julius Caesar* performed at the Globe:

> The playhouses are so constructed that they play on a raised platform, so that everyone has a good view. There are different galleries and places [*orchestra, sedilia, porticus*], however, where the seating is better and more comfortable and therefore more expensive. For whoever cares to stand below only pays one English penny, but if he wishes to sit, he enters by another door [*ingressus*] and pays another penny, while if he desires to sit in the most comfortable seats, which are cushioned, where he not only sees everything well but can also be seen, then he pays yet another English penny at another door. And during the performance food and drink are carried round the audience, so that for what one cares to pay one may also have refreshment.

Scenery was not used, though the theater building itself was handsome enough to invoke a feeling of order and hierarchy that lent itself to the splendor and pageantry onstage. Portable properties, such as thrones, stools, tables, and beds, could be carried or thrust on as needed. In the scene pictured here by de Witt, a lady on a bench, attended perhaps by her waiting-gentlewoman, receives the address of a male figure. If Shakespeare had written *Twelfth Night* by 1596 for performance at the Swan, we could imagine Malvolio appearing like this as he bows before the Countess Olivia and her gentlewoman, Maria.

MACBETH

Three WITCHES *or* WEIRD SISTERS
HECATE
Three APPARITIONS

Lords, Gentlemen, Officers, Soldiers, Murderers, and
  Attendants

SCENE: *Scotland; England*]

1.1   *Thunder and lightning. Enter three Witches.*

FIRST WITCH
  When shall we three meet again?
  In thunder, lightning, or in rain?   2
SECOND WITCH
  When the hurlyburly's done,   3
  When the battle's lost and won.
THIRD WITCH
  That will be ere the set of sun.
FIRST WITCH
  Where the place?
SECOND WITCH   Upon the heath.
THIRD WITCH
  There to meet with Macbeth.
FIRST WITCH   I come, Grimalkin!   8
SECOND WITCH   Paddock calls.   9
THIRD WITCH   Anon.   10
ALL
  Fair is foul, and foul is fair.
  Hover through the fog and filthy air.   *Exeunt.*

❖

1.2   *Alarum within. Enter King [Duncan], Malcolm,
          Donalbain, Lennox, with attendants, meeting a
          bleeding Captain.*

DUNCAN
  What bloody man is that? He can report,
  As seemeth by his plight, of the revolt
  The newest state.
MALCOLM   This is the sergeant   3

1.1. Location: An open place.
2 In thunder . . . rain (Witches were thought able to choose and localize
the storms about them.)   **3 hurlyburly** tumult   **8 Grimalkin** i.e., gray
cat, name of the witch's familiar spirit   **9 Paddock** toad; also a familiar   **10 Anon** at once, right away

1.2. Location: A camp near Forres.
s.d. Alarum trumpet call to arms   **3 sergeant** i.e., staff officer. (There
may be no inconsistency with his rank of "captain" in the stage direction and speech prefixes in the Folio.)

Who like a good and hardy soldier fought
'Gainst my captivity. Hail, brave friend!
Say to the King the knowledge of the broil   6
As thou didst leave it.

CAPTAIN   Doubtful it stood,
As two spent swimmers that do cling together   8
And choke their art. The merciless Macdonwald—   9
Worthy to be a rebel, for to that   10
The multiplying villainies of nature   11
Do swarm upon him—from the Western Isles   12
Of kerns and gallowglasses is supplied;   13
And Fortune, on his damnèd quarrel smiling,   14
Showed like a rebel's whore. But all's too weak;   15
For brave Macbeth—well he deserves that name—   16
Disdaining Fortune, with his brandished steel,
Which smoked with bloody execution,
Like valor's minion carved out his passage   19
Till he faced the slave,   20
Which ne'er shook hands nor bade farewell to him   21
Till he unseamed him from the nave to the chops,   22
And fixed his head upon our battlements.

DUNCAN
O valiant cousin, worthy gentleman!   24

CAPTAIN
As whence the sun 'gins his reflection   25
Shipwrecking storms and direful thunders break,   26
So from that spring whence comfort seemed to come   27
Discomfort swells. Mark, King of Scotland, mark.   28
No sooner justice had, with valor armed,

---

6 broil battle   **8 spent** tired out   **9 choke their art** render their skill in
swimming useless   **10 to that** as if to that end or purpose   **11–12 The
multiplying . . . him** i.e., ever-increasing numbers of villainous rebels
swarm about him like vermin   **12 Western Isles** islands to the west of
Scotland, the Hebrides and perhaps Ireland   **13 Of kerns** with light-
armed Irish foot soldiers.   **gallowglasses** horsemen armed with axes
14 quarrel cause, claim   **15 Showed** appeared   **16 name** i.e., "brave"
19 minion darling   **20 the slave** i.e., Macdonwald   **21 Which** who, i.e.,
Macbeth.   **ne'er . . . to him** i.e., proffered no polite salutation or farewell, acted without ceremony   **22 nave** navel.   **chops** jaws   **24 cousin**
kinsman   **25 As whence** just as from the place where.   **'gins his reflection** begins its turning back (from its southward progression during
winter)   **26 break** break forth, emanate   **27 spring** (1) the season of
spring (2) source   **28 swells** wells up

Compelled these skipping kerns to trust their heels   30
But the Norweyan lord, surveying vantage,   31
With furbished arms and new supplies of men,
Began a fresh assault.

DUNCAN
Dismayed not this our captains, Macbeth and Banquo?

CAPTAIN
Yes, as sparrows eagles, or the hare the lion.
If I say sooth, I must report they were   36
As cannons overcharged with double cracks,   37
So they doubly redoubled strokes upon the foe.   38
Except they meant to bathe in reeking wounds   39
Or memorize another Golgotha,   40
I cannot tell.
But I am faint. My gashes cry for help.

DUNCAN
So well thy words become thee as thy wounds;
They smack of honor both.—Go get him surgeons.
                     [*Exit Captain, attended.*]

Enter Ross and Angus.

Who comes here?

MALCOLM   The worthy Thane of Ross.   45

LENNOX   What a haste looks through his eyes!
So should he look that seems to speak things strange.   47

ROSS   God save the King!

DUNCAN   Whence cam'st thou, worthy thane?

ROSS   From Fife, great King,
Where the Norweyan banners flout the sky   51
And fan our people cold.   52
Norway himself, with terrible numbers,   53
Assisted by that most disloyal traitor,
The Thane of Cawdor, began a dismal conflict,   55

---

30 skipping (1) lightly armed, quick at maneuvering (2) skittish
31 surveying vantage seeing an opportunity   **36 say sooth** tell the
truth   **37 cracks** charges of explosive   **38 So** in such a way that
39 Except unless   **40 memorize** make memorable or famous.   **Golgotha**
"place of a skull," where Christ was crucified. (Mark 15:22.)   **45 Thane**
Scottish title of honor, roughly equivalent to "Earl"   **47 seems to** seems
about to   **51 flout** mock, insult   **52 fan . . . cold** fan cold fear into our
troops   **53 Norway** the King of Norway   **55 dismal** ominous

Till that Bellona's bridegroom, lapped in proof,   56
Confronted him with self-comparisons,   57
Point against point, rebellious arm 'gainst arm,
Curbing his lavish spirit; and to conclude,   59
The victory fell on us.

DUNCAN   Great happiness!

ROSS   That now
Sweno, the Norways' king, craves composition;   62
Nor would we deign him burial of his men
Till he disbursèd at Saint Colme's Inch   64
Ten thousand dollars to our general use.   65

DUNCAN
No more that Thane of Cawdor shall deceive
Our bosom interest. Go pronounce his present death,   67
And with his former title greet Macbeth.

ROSS   I'll see it done.

DUNCAN
What he hath lost noble Macbeth hath won.

                                        Exeunt.

❖

1.3   *Thunder. Enter the three Witches.*

FIRST WITCH   Where hast thou been, sister?
SECOND WITCH   Killing swine.
THIRD WITCH   Sister, where thou?
FIRST WITCH
A sailor's wife had chestnuts in her lap,
And munched, and munched, and munched. "Give me,"
    quoth I.
"Aroint thee, witch!" the rump-fed runnion cries.   6

---

56 Till . . . proof i.e., until Macbeth, clad in well-tested armor. (Bellona
was the Roman goddess of war.)   **57 him** i.e., the King of Norway.   **self-
comparisons** i.e., matching counterthrusts   **59 lavish** insolent, unrestrained   **62 Norways'** Norwegians'.   **composition** agreement, treaty of
peace   **64 Saint Colme's Inch** Inchcolm, the Isle of St. Columba in the
Firth of Forth   **65 dollars** Spanish or Dutch coins   **67 Our** (The royal
"we.")   **bosom** close and affectionate.   **present** immediate

1.3. Location: A heath near Forres.
6 Aroint thee avaunt, begone.   **rump-fed** fed on refuse, or fat-rumped.
runnion mangy creature, scabby woman

Her husband's to Aleppo gone, master o' the *Tiger*;   7
But in a sieve I'll thither sail,
And like a rat without a tail   9
I'll do, I'll do, and I'll do.

SECOND WITCH
I'll give thee a wind.

FIRST WITCH
Thou'rt kind.

THIRD WITCH
And I another.

FIRST WITCH
I myself have all the other,
And the very ports they blow,   15
All the quarters that they know
I' the shipman's card.   17
I'll drain him dry as hay.
Sleep shall neither night nor day
Hang upon his penthouse lid.   20
He shall live a man forbid.   21
Weary sev'nnights nine times nine   22
Shall he dwindle, peak, and pine.   23
Though his bark cannot be lost,
Yet it shall be tempest-tossed.
Look what I have.

SECOND WITCH   Show me, show me.

FIRST WITCH
Here I have a pilot's thumb,
Wrecked as homeward he did come.   *Drum within.*

THIRD WITCH
A drum, a drum!
Macbeth doth come.

ALL [*Dancing in a circle*]
The Weird Sisters, hand in hand,   32

---

7 Tiger (A ship's name.)   **9 like** in the shape of.   **without a tail** (A familiar, or transformed witch, was thought to be recognizable by some bodily defect. The missing tail here, suggestive of a generative defect and hence of futility, introduces a sexual pun on *do*, l. 10.)   **15 they blow** i.e., from which the winds blow. (The witches can prevent a ship from entering port this way.)   **17 shipman's card** compass card, or a chart **20 penthouse lid** i.e., eyelid (which projects out over the eye like a *penthouse* or slope-roofed structure)   **21 forbid** accursed   **22 sev'nnights** weeks   **23 peak** grow peaked or thin   **32 Weird** connected with fate

Posters of the sea and land,   33
Thus do go about, about,
Thrice to thine, and thrice to mine,
And thrice again, to make up nine.
Peace! The charm's wound up.

Enter Macbeth and Banquo.

MACBETH
So foul and fair a day I have not seen.
BANQUO
How far is 't called to Forres?—What are these,   39
So withered and so wild in their attire,
That look not like th' inhabitants o' th' earth
And yet are on 't?—Live you? Or are you aught
That man may question? You seem to understand me
By each at once her chappy finger laying   44
Upon her skinny lips. You should be women,
And yet your beards forbid me to interpret
That you are so.
MACBETH   Speak, if you can. What are you?
FIRST WITCH
All hail, Macbeth! Hail to thee, Thane of Glamis!
SECOND WITCH
All hail, Macbeth! Hail to thee, Thane of Cawdor!
THIRD WITCH
All hail, Macbeth, that shalt be king hereafter!
BANQUO
Good sir, why do you start and seem to fear
Things that do sound so fair?—I' the name of truth,
Are ye fantastical or that indeed   53
Which outwardly ye show? My noble partner   54
You greet with present grace and great prediction   55
Of noble having and of royal hope,
That he seems rapt withal. To me you speak not.   57
If you can look into the seeds of time
And say which grain will grow and which will not,

33 **Posters of** swift travelers over   39 **is 't called** is it said to be
44 **chappy** chapped   53 **fantastical** creatures of fantasy or imagination   54 **show** appear   55 **grace** honor   57 **rapt** carried away (by
thought).   **withal** with it, by it

Speak then to me, who neither beg nor fear   60
Your favors nor your hate.   61

FIRST WITCH   Hail!

SECOND WITCH   Hail!

THIRD WITCH   Hail!

FIRST WITCH
Lesser than Macbeth, and greater.

SECOND WITCH
Not so happy, yet much happier.   66

THIRD WITCH
Thou shalt get kings, though thou be none.   67
So all hail, Macbeth and Banquo!

FIRST WITCH
Banquo and Macbeth, all hail!

MACBETH
Stay, you imperfect speakers, tell me more!   70
By Sinel's death I know I am Thane of Glamis,   71
But how of Cawdor? The Thane of Cawdor lives
A prosperous gentleman; and to be king
Stands not within the prospect of belief,
No more than to be Cawdor. Say from whence
You owe this strange intelligence, or why   76
Upon this blasted heath you stop our way   77
With such prophetic greeting? Speak, I charge you.
                       Witches vanish.

BANQUO
The earth hath bubbles, as the water has,
And these are of them. Whither are they vanished?

MACBETH
Into the air; and what seemed corporal melted,   81
As breath into the wind. Would they had stayed!

BANQUO
Were such things here as we do speak about?
Or have we eaten on the insane root   84
That takes the reason prisoner?

60–61 beg . . . hate beg your favors nor fear your hate   **66 happy** fortunate   **67 get** beget   **70 imperfect** incomplete   **71 Sinel's** (Sinel was Macbeth's father.)   **76 owe** own, possess.   **strange** (1) unusual (2) unnatural, frighteningly alien to human experience (as often elsewhere in this play).   **intelligence** news   **77 blasted** blighted   **81 corporal** bodily   **84 on** of.   **insane root** root causing insanity; variously identified

MACBETH
Your children shall be kings.

BANQUO   You shall be king.

MACBETH
And Thane of Cawdor too. Went it not so?

BANQUO
To th' selfsame tune and words.—Who's here?

    Enter Ross and Angus.

ROSS
The King hath happily received, Macbeth,
The news of thy success; and when he reads   90
Thy personal venture in the rebels' sight,   91
His wonders and his praises do contend   92
Which should be thine or his. Silenced with that,   93
In viewing o'er the rest o' the selfsame day
He finds thee in the stout Norweyan ranks,
Nothing afeard of what thyself didst make,   96
Strange images of death. As thick as tale   97
Came post with post, and every one did bear   98
Thy praises in his kingdom's great defense,
And poured them down before him.

ANGUS   We are sent
To give thee from our royal master thanks,
Only to herald thee into his sight,
Not pay thee.

ROSS
And, for an earnest of a greater honor,   104
He bade me, from him, call thee Thane of Cawdor;
In which addition, hail, most worthy thane,   106
For it is thine.

BANQUO   What, can the devil speak true?

MACBETH
The Thane of Cawdor lives. Why do you dress me
In borrowed robes?

ANGUS   Who was the thane lives yet,   109

90 reads i.e., considers   **91 Thy . . . sight** your endangering yourself
before the very eyes of the rebels   **92–93 His . . . that** i.e., your won-
drous deeds so outdo any praise he could offer that he is silenced
96 Nothing not at all   **97–98 As . . . with post** as fast as could be told,
i.e., counted, came messenger after messenger   **104 earnest** token
payment   **106 addition** title   **109 Who** he who

But under heavy judgment bears that life
Which he deserves to lose. Whether he was combined 111
With those of Norway, or did line the rebel   112
With hidden help and vantage, or that with both
He labored in his country's wrack, I know not;   114
But treasons capital, confessed and proved,   115
Have overthrown him.

MACBETH [*Aside*]   Glamis, and Thane of Cawdor!
The greatest is behind. [*To Ross and Angus.*] Thanks for
    your pains.   117
[*Aside to Banquo.*] Do you not hope your children shall
    be kings
When those that gave the Thane of Cawdor to me
Promised no less to them?

BANQUO [*To Macbeth*]   That, trusted home,   120
Might yet enkindle you unto the crown,
Besides the Thane of Cawdor. But 'tis strange;
And oftentimes to win us to our harm
The instruments of darkness tell us truths,   124
Win us with honest trifles, to betray 's
In deepest consequence.—   126
Cousins, a word, I pray you.   127
          [*He converses apart with Ross and Angus.*]

MACBETH [*Aside*]   Two truths are told,
As happy prologues to the swelling act   129
Of the imperial theme.—I thank you, gentlemen.
[*Aside.*] This supernatural soliciting   131
Cannot be ill, cannot be good. If ill,
Why hath it given me earnest of success
Commencing in a truth? I am Thane of Cawdor.
If good, why do I yield to that suggestion
Whose horrid image doth unfix my hair   136
And make my seated heart knock at my ribs,
Against the use of nature? Present fears   138

---

111 combined confederate   **112 line** strengthen.   **the rebel** i.e., Macdonwald   **114 in** i.e., to bring about.   **wrack** ruin   **115 capital** deserving death   **117 behind** to come   **120 home** all the way   **124 darkness**
(Indicates the demonic beyond the witches.)   **126 In deepest consequence** in the profoundly important sequel   **127 Cousins** i.e., fellow
lords   **129 swelling act** stately drama   **131 soliciting** tempting
136 horrid literally, "bristling," like Macbeth's hair   **138 use** custom.
fears things feared

Are less than horrible imaginings.
My thought, whose murder yet is but fantastical,   140
Shakes so my single state of man   141
That function is smothered in surmise,   142
And nothing is but what is not.   143

BANQUO   Look how our partner's rapt.

MACBETH [*Aside*]
If chance will have me king, why, chance may crown me
Without my stir.

BANQUO   New honors come upon him,   146
Like our strange garments, cleave not to their mold   147
But with the aid of use.

MACBETH [*Aside*]   Come what come may,
Time and the hour runs through the roughest day.   149

BANQUO
Worthy Macbeth, we stay upon your leisure.   150

MACBETH
Give me your favor. My dull brain was wrought   151
With things forgotten. Kind gentlemen, your pains
Are registered where every day I turn   153
The leaf to read them. Let us toward the King.
[*Aside to Banquo.*] Think upon what hath chanced, and
at more time,   155
The interim having weighed it, let us speak
Our free hearts each to other.   157

BANQUO [*To Macbeth*]   Very gladly.

MACBETH [*To Banquo*]   Till then, enough.—Come, friends.
                         Exeunt.

❖

140 whose in which.   **but fantastical** merely imagined   **141 single . . .
man** weak human condition   **142 function** normal power of action.
surmise speculation, imaginings   **143 nothing . . . not** only unreal
imaginings have (for me) any reality   **146 stir** bestirring (myself).   **come**
i.e., which have come   **147 strange** unaccustomed (with an ironical
glance at "alien").   **their mold** i.e., the shape of the person within
them   **149 Time . . . day** i.e., what must happen will happen one way or
another   **150 stay** wait   **151 favor** pardon   **153 registered** recorded (in
my memory)   **155 at more time** at a time of greater leisure   **157 Our
free hearts** our hearts freely

1.4   *Flourish. Enter King [Duncan], Lennox,*
        Malcolm, Donalbain, and attendants.

DUNCAN
   Is execution done on Cawdor? Are not
   Those in commission yet returned?

MALCOLM   My liege,   2
   They are not yet come back. But I have spoke
   With one that saw him die, who did report
   That very frankly he confessed his treasons,
   Implored Your Highness' pardon, and set forth
   A deep repentance. Nothing in his life
   Became him like the leaving it. He died
   As one that had been studied in his death   9
   To throw away the dearest thing he owed   10
   As 'twere a careless trifle.

DUNCAN   There's no art   11
   To find the mind's construction in the face.
   He was a gentleman on whom I built
   An absolute trust.

     Enter Macbeth, Banquo, Ross, and Angus.

           O worthiest cousin!
   The sin of my ingratitude even now
   Was heavy on me. Thou art so far before   16
   That swiftest wing of recompense is slow
   To overtake thee. Would thou hadst less deserved,
   That the proportion both of thanks and payment   19
   Might have been mine! Only I have left to say,   20
   More is thy due than more than all can pay.

MACBETH
   The service and the loyalty I owe,
   In doing it, pays itself. Your Highness' part
   Is to receive our duties; and our duties
   Are to your throne and state children and servants,   25

1.4. Location: Forres. The palace.
2 in commission having warrant (to see to the execution of Cawdor)
9 been studied made it his study   **10 owed** owned   **11 careless** uncared
for   **16 before** ahead (in deserving)   **19–20 That . . . mine** i.e., that I
might have thanked and rewarded you in ample proportion to your
worth   **25 Are . . . servants** i.e., are like children and servants in relation
to your throne and dignity, existing only to serve you

Which do but what they should by doing everything
Safe toward your love and honor.

DUNCAN   Welcome hither!   27
I have begun to plant thee, and will labor
To make thee full of growing. Noble Banquo,
That hast no less deserved, nor must be known
No less to have done so, let me infold thee
And hold thee to my heart.

BANQUO   There if I grow,
The harvest is your own.

DUNCAN   My plenteous joys,
Wanton in fullness, seek to hide themselves   34
In drops of sorrow.—Sons, kinsmen, thanes,
And you whose places are the nearest, know
We will establish our estate upon   37
Our eldest, Malcolm, whom we name hereafter
The Prince of Cumberland; which honor must   39
Not unaccompanied invest him only,   40
But signs of nobleness, like stars, shall shine
On all deservers.—From hence to Inverness,   42
And bind us further to you.   43

MACBETH
The rest is labor which is not used for you.   44
I'll be myself the harbinger and make joyful   45
The hearing of my wife with your approach;
So humbly take my leave.

DUNCAN   My worthy Cawdor!

MACBETH [*Aside*]
The Prince of Cumberland! That is a step
On which I must fall down or else o'erleap,
For in my way it lies. Stars, hide your fires;   50

---

27 Safe toward to safeguard   **34 Wanton** unrestrained   **37 We** (The royal
"we.")   **establish our estate** fix the succession of our state   **39 Prince
of Cumberland** title of the heir apparent to the Scottish throne   **40 Not
. . . only** i.e., not be bestowed on Malcolm alone; other deserving nobles
are to share honors   **42 Inverness** the seat or location of Macbeth's
castle, Dunsinane   **43 bind . . . you** i.e., put me further in your (Macbeth's) obligation by your hospitality   **44 The . . . you** i.e., even repose,
when not devoted to your service, becomes tedious and wearisome
45 harbinger forerunner, messenger to arrange royal lodging   **50 in my
way it lies** (The monarchy was not hereditary, and Macbeth had a right
to believe that he himself might be chosen as Duncan's successor; he
here questions whether he will interfere with the course of events.)

Let not light see my black and deep desires.
The eye wink at the hand; yet let that be　　　　　52
Which the eye fears, when it is done, to see.　　　*Exit.*

DUNCAN
True, worthy Banquo. He is full so valiant,　　　　54
And in his commendations I am fed;
It is a banquet to me. Let's after him,
Whose care is gone before to bid us welcome.
It is a peerless kinsman.　　　　*Flourish. Exeunt.*

❖

1.5　　*Enter Macbeth's Wife, alone, with a letter.*

LADY MACBETH [*Reads*] "They met me in the day of
success; and I have learned by the perfect'st report they　2
have more in them than mortal knowledge. When I
burnt in desire to question them further, they made
themselves air, into which they vanished. Whiles I
stood rapt in the wonder of it came missives from the　6
King, who all-hailed me 'Thane of Cawdor,' by which
title, before, these Weird Sisters saluted me, and referred me to the coming on of time with 'Hail, king
that shalt be!' This have I thought good to deliver thee,　10
my dearest partner of greatness, that thou mightst not
lose the dues of rejoicing by being ignorant of what
greatness is promised thee. Lay it to thy heart, and
farewell."
Glamis thou art, and Cawdor, and shalt be
What thou art promised. Yet do I fear thy nature;　　16
It is too full o' the milk of human kindness
To catch the nearest way. Thou wouldst be great,
Art not without ambition, but without
The illness should attend it. What thou wouldst highly,　20
That wouldst thou holily; wouldst not play false,
And yet wouldst wrongly win. Thou'dst have, great
　Glamis,

---

52 wink . . . hand blind itself to the hand's deed.　**let that be** may that
thing come to pass　**54 full so valiant** fully as valiant as you say

1.5. Location: Inverness. Macbeth's castle.
2 perfect'st most accurate　**6 missives** messengers　**10 deliver** inform
16 fear am anxious about, mistrust　**20 illness** evil (which).　**highly** greatly

That which cries "Thus thou must do," if thou have it, 23
And that which rather thou dost fear to do 24
Than wishest should be undone. Hie thee hither, 25
That I may pour my spirits in thine ear
And chastise with the valor of my tongue
All that impedes thee from the golden round 28
Which fate and metaphysical aid doth seem 29
To have thee crowned withal.

Enter Messenger.

What is your tidings? 30
MESSENGER
The King comes here tonight.
LADY MACBETH   Thou'rt mad to say it!
Is not thy master with him, who, were 't so,
Would have informed for preparation? 33
MESSENGER
So please you, it is true. Our thane is coming.
One of my fellows had the speed of him, 35
Who, almost dead for breath, had scarcely more
Than would make up his message.
LADY MACBETH   Give him tending; 37
He brings great news.   *Exit Messenger.*
The raven himself is hoarse
That croaks the fatal entrance of Duncan
Under my battlements. Come, you spirits
That tend on mortal thoughts, unsex me here 41
And fill me from the crown to the toe top-full
Of direst cruelty! Make thick my blood;
Stop up th' access and passage to remorse, 44
That no compunctious visitings of nature 45
Shake my fell purpose, nor keep peace between 46

---

23 have are to have, want to have   **24–25 And that . . . undone** i.e., and
the thing you ambitiously crave frightens you more in terms of the
means needed to achieve it than in the idea of having it; if you could
have it without those means, you certainly wouldn't wish it undone
25 Hie hasten   **28 round** crown   **29 metaphysical** supernatural
30 withal with   **33 informed for preparation** i.e., sent me word so that I
might get things ready   **35 had . . . of** outstripped   **37 tending** atten-
dance   **41 tend . . . thoughts** attend on, act as the instruments of deadly
or murderous thoughts   **44 remorse** pity   **45 nature** natural feelings
46 fell fierce, cruel.   **keep peace** intervene

Th' effect and it! Come to my woman's breasts   47
And take my milk for gall, you murdering ministers,   48
Wherever in your sightless substances   49
You wait on nature's mischief! Come, thick night,   50
And pall thee in the dunnest smoke of hell,   51
That my keen knife see not the wound it makes,
Nor heaven peep through the blanket of the dark
To cry "Hold, hold!"

    Enter Macbeth.

                Great Glamis! Worthy Cawdor!
Greater than both by the all-hail hereafter!
Thy letters have transported me beyond   56
This ignorant present, and I feel now
The future in the instant.
MACBETH   My dearest love,
Duncan comes here tonight.
LADY MACBETH   And when goes hence?
MACBETH
Tomorrow, as he purposes.
LADY MACBETH   O, never
Shall sun that morrow see!
Your face, my thane, is as a book where men
May read strange matters. To beguile the time,   63
Look like the time; bear welcome in your eye,   64
Your hand, your tongue. Look like th' innocent flower,
But be the serpent under 't. He that's coming
Must be provided for; and you shall put
This night's great business into my dispatch,   68
Which shall to all our nights and days to come
Give solely sovereign sway and masterdom.
MACBETH
We will speak further.
LADY MACBETH   Only look up clear.   71

---

47 Th' effect and it i.e., my *fell purpose* and its accomplishment   **48 for gall** in exchange for gall.   **ministers** agents   **49 sightless** invisible   **50 wait on** attend, assist.   **nature's mischief** evil done to nature, or within the realm of nature   **51 pall** envelop.   **dunnest** darkest   **56 letters have** i.e., letter has   **63 beguile the time** i.e., deceive all observers   **64 Look like the time** look the way people expect you to look   **68 dispatch** management   **71 look up clear** give the appearance of being untroubled

To alter favor ever is to fear.   72
Leave all the rest to me.   *Exeunt.*

❖

1.6   *Hautboys and torches. Enter King [Duncan],*
          Malcolm, Donalbain, Banquo, Lennox,
          Macduff, Ross, Angus, and attendants.

DUNCAN
  This castle hath a pleasant seat. The air   1
  Nimbly and sweetly recommends itself
  Unto our gentle senses.
BANQUO   This guest of summer,   3
  The temple-haunting martlet, does approve   4
  By his loved mansionry that the heaven's breath   5
  Smells wooingly here. No jutty, frieze,   6
  Buttress, nor coign of vantage but this bird   7
  Hath made his pendent bed and procreant cradle.   8
  Where they most breed and haunt, I have observed
  The air is delicate.

      Enter Lady [Macbeth].

DUNCAN   See, see, our honored hostess!
  The love that follows us sometimes is our trouble,   11
  Which still we thank as love. Herein I teach you   12
  How you shall bid God 'ild us for your pains,   13
  And thank us for your trouble.
LADY MACBETH   All our service
  In every point twice done, and then done double,

---

72 **To . . . fear** to show a troubled countenance is to arouse suspicion

1.6. Location: Before Macbeth's castle.
s.d. Hautboys oboelike instruments   **1 seat** site   **3 gentle** (1) noble
(2) delicate (applied to the air)   **4 temple-haunting** nesting in
churches.   **martlet** house martin.   **approve** prove   **5 mansionry** nest-
building   **6 jutty** projection of wall or building   **7 coign of vantage**
convenient corner, i.e., for nesting   **8 procreant** for breeding
11–12 The love . . . love i.e., the love that sometimes forces itself incon-
veniently upon us we still appreciate, since it is meant as love. (Duncan
is graciously suggesting that his visit is a bother, but, he hopes, a
welcome one.)   **13 bid . . . pains** ask God to reward me for the trouble
I'm giving you. (This is said in the same gently jocose spirit as ll. 11–12.)

Were poor and single business to contend   16
Against those honors deep and broad wherewith   17
Your Majesty loads our house. For those of old,   18
And the late dignities heaped up to them,   19
We rest your hermits.

DUNCAN   Where's the Thane of Cawdor?   20
We coursed him at the heels, and had a purpose   21
To be his purveyor; but he rides well,   22
And his great love, sharp as his spur, hath holp him   23
To his home before us. Fair and noble hostess,
We are your guest tonight.

LADY MACBETH   Your servants ever
Have theirs, themselves, and what is theirs in compt   26
To make their audit at Your Highness' pleasure,   27
Still to return your own.

DUNCAN   Give me your hand.   28
Conduct me to mine host. We love him highly,   29
And shall continue our graces towards him.
By your leave, hostess.   *Exeunt.*

❖

1.7   *Hautboys. Torches. Enter a sewer, and divers*
      servants with dishes and service, [and pass]
      over the stage. Then enter Macbeth.

MACBETH
If it were done when 'tis done, then 'twere well
It were done quickly. If th' assassination

---

16 single small, inconsiderable   **16–17 contend Against** vie with
18 those of old i.e., honors formerly bestowed on us   **19 late** recent.
to besides, in addition to   **20 rest** remain.   **hermits** i.e., those who will
pray for you like hermits or beadsmen   **21 coursed** followed (as in a
hunt)   **22 purveyor** an officer sent ahead to provide for entertainment;
here, forerunner   **23 holp** helped   **26 Have theirs** i.e., have their servants.   **what is theirs** their wealth, possessions.   **in compt** in trust,
under obligation (to serve the King)   **27 make their audit** render their
account   **28 Still** always.   **return your own** i.e., merely render back
what is yours, since we hold it in trust from you   **29 We** (The royal
"we.")

1.7. Location: Macbeth's castle; an inner courtyard.
s.d. sewer chief waiter, butler

Could trammel up the consequence and catch   3
With his surcease success—that but this blow   4
Might be the be-all and the end-all!—here,   5
But here, upon this bank and shoal of time,
We'd jump the life to come. But in these cases   7
We still have judgment here, that we but teach   8
Bloody instructions, which, being taught, return   9
To plague th' inventor. This evenhanded justice
Commends th' ingredience of our poisoned chalice   11
To our own lips. He's here in double trust:
First, as I am his kinsman and his subject,
Strong both against the deed; then, as his host,
Who should against his murderer shut the door,
Not bear the knife myself. Besides, this Duncan
Hath borne his faculties so meek, hath been   17
So clear in his great office, that his virtues   18
Will plead like angels, trumpet-tongued, against
The deep damnation of his taking-off;   20
And Pity, like a naked newborn babe
Striding the blast, or heaven's cherubin, horsed   22
Upon the sightless couriers of the air,   23
Shall blow the horrid deed in every eye,
That tears shall drown the wind. I have no spur   25
To prick the sides of my intent, but only
Vaulting ambition, which o'erleaps itself
And falls on th' other—   28

    Enter Lady [*Macbeth*].

How now, what news?

LADY MACBETH
He has almost supped. Why have you left the chamber?

3 **trammel . . . consequence** entangle in a net and prevent the resulting
events   4 **his surcease** cessation (of the assassination and of Duncan's
life).   **success** what succeeds, follows   5 **here** in this world   7 **jump**
risk. (But imaging the physical act is characteristic of Macbeth; cf.
l. 27.)   8 **still have judgment** are invariably punished.   **that** in that
9 **instructions** lessons   11 **Commends** presents.   **ingredience** contents
of a mixture   17 **faculties** powers of office   18 **clear** free of taint
20 **taking-off** murder   22 **Striding** bestriding   23 **sightless couriers**
invisible steeds or runners, i.e., the winds   25 **shall drown the wind** i.e.,
will be as heavy as a downpour of rain, which is thought to still the
wind   28 **other** other side. (The image is of a horseman vaulting into his
saddle and ignominiously falling on the opposite side.)

MACBETH
　Hath he asked for me?
LADY MACBETH　　　　　Know you not he has?
MACBETH
　We will proceed no further in this business.
　He hath honored me of late, and I have bought　　33
　Golden opinions from all sorts of people,
　Which would be worn now in their newest gloss,　　35
　Not cast aside so soon.
LADY MACBETH　　　　　Was the hope drunk
　Wherein you dressed yourself? Hath it slept since?
　And wakes it now, to look so green and pale　　38
　At what it did so freely? From this time
　Such I account thy love. Art thou afeard
　To be the same in thine own act and valor
　As thou art in desire? Wouldst thou have that
　Which thou esteem'st the ornament of life,　　43
　And live a coward in thine own esteem,
　Letting "I dare not" wait upon "I would,"　　45
　Like the poor cat i' th' adage?
MACBETH　　　　　Prithee, peace!　　46
　I dare do all that may become a man;
　Who dares do more is none.
LADY MACBETH　　　　　What beast was 't, then,
　That made you break this enterprise to me?　　49
　When you durst do it, then you were a man;
　And to be more than what you were, you would
　Be so much more the man. Nor time nor place
　Did then adhere, and yet you would make both.　　53
　They have made themselves, and that their fitness now　54
　Does unmake you. I have given suck, and know
　How tender 'tis to love the babe that milks me;
　I would, while it was smiling in my face,
　Have plucked my nipple from his boneless gums
　And dashed the brains out, had I so sworn as you
　Have done to this.
MACBETH　　　　　If we should fail?

33 **bought** acquired (by bravery in battle)　35 **would** ought to, want to
38 **green** sickly　43 **the ornament of life** i.e., the crown　45 **wait upon**
accompany, attend　46 **adage** (i.e., "The cat would eat fish, and would
not wet her feet")　49 **break** broach　53 **adhere** agree, suit.　**would**
wanted to　54 **that their fitness** their very suitability

LADY MACBETH   We fail?
But screw your courage to the sticking place   61
And we'll not fail. When Duncan is asleep—
Whereto the rather shall his day's hard journey
Soundly invite him—his two chamberlains   64
Will I with wine and wassail so convince   65
That memory, the warder of the brain,   66
Shall be a fume, and the receipt of reason   67
A limbeck only. When in swinish sleep   68
Their drenchèd natures lies as in a death,
What cannot you and I perform upon
Th' unguarded Duncan? What not put upon
His spongy officers, who shall bear the guilt   72
Of our great quell?
MACBETH   Bring forth men-children only!   73
For thy undaunted mettle should compose   74
Nothing but males. Will it not be received,   75
When we have marked with blood those sleepy two
Of his own chamber and used their very daggers,
That they have done 't?
LADY MACBETH   Who dares receive it other,   78
As we shall make our griefs and clamor roar   79
Upon his death?
MACBETH   I am settled, and bend up   80
Each corporal agent to this terrible feat.   81
Away, and mock the time with fairest show.   82
False face must hide what the false heart doth know.

Exeunt.

❖

61 But only.   **the sticking place** the notch into which is fitted the string
of a crossbow cranked taut for shooting   **64 chamberlains** attendants
on the bedchamber   **65 wassail** carousal, drink.   **convince** overpower
66–68 warder . . . only (The brain was thought to be divided into three
ventricles, imagination in front, memory at the back, and between them
the seat of reason. The fumes of wine, arising from the stomach, would
deaden memory and judgment.)   **67 receipt** receptacle, ventricle
68 limbeck alembic, still   **72 spongy** soaked, drunken   **73 quell** murder   **74 mettle** temperament   **75 received** i.e., as truth   **78 other**
otherwise   **79 As** inasmuch as   **80–81 bend . . . agent** strain every
muscle   **82 mock** deceive

2.1   *Enter Banquo, and Fleance, with a torch before him.*

BANQUO   How goes the night, boy?

FLEANCE
The moon is down. I have not heard the clock.

BANQUO
And she goes down at twelve.

FLEANCE   I take 't 'tis later, sir.

BANQUO
Hold, take my sword. [*He gives him his sword.*] There's
husbandry in heaven;   4
Their candles are all out. Take thee that too.
                              [*He gives him his belt and dagger.*]
A heavy summons lies like lead upon me,   6
And yet I would not sleep. Merciful powers,   7
Restrain in me the cursèd thoughts that nature
Gives way to in repose!

   Enter Macbeth, and a servant with a torch.

Give me my sword. Who's there? [*He takes his sword.*]

MACBETH   A friend.

BANQUO
What, sir, not yet at rest? The King's abed.
He hath been in unusual pleasure,
And sent forth great largess to your offices.   14
This diamond he greets your wife withal,
By the name of most kind hostess, and shut up   16
In measureless content.   [*He gives a diamond.*]

MACBETH   Being unprepared,   17
Our will became the servant to defect,   18
Which else should free have wrought.   19

**2.1. Location: Inner courtyard of Macbeth's castle. Time is virtually
continuous from the previous scene.**
s.d. torch (This may mean "torchbearer," although it does not at l. 9
s.d.)   **4 husbandry** economy   **6 summons** i.e., to sleep   **7 would not** do
not wish to.   **powers** order of angels deputed by God to resist demons
14 largess gifts, gratuities.   **offices** quarters used for the household
work   **16–17 shut up In** concluded what he had to say with expressions
of; or, perhaps, he professes himself enclosed in   **18 Our . . . defect** our
good will (to entertain the King handsomely) was limited by our meager
means (at such short notice)   **19 free** freely, unrestrainedly

BANQUO   All's well.
   I dreamt last night of the three Weird Sisters.
   To you they have showed some truth.
MACBETH   I think not of them.
   Yet, when we can entreat an hour to serve,
   We would spend it in some words upon that business,
   If you would grant the time.
BANQUO   At your kind'st leisure.
MACBETH
   If you shall cleave to my consent when 'tis,   26
   It shall make honor for you.
BANQUO   So I lose none   27
   In seeking to augment it, but still keep
   My bosom franchised and allegiance clear,   29
   I shall be counseled.
MACBETH   Good repose the while!   30
BANQUO   Thanks, sir. The like to you.
                           Exit Banquo [with Fleance].

MACBETH
   Go bid thy mistress, when my drink is ready,   32
   She strike upon the bell. Get thee to bed.
                                  Exit [Servant].
   Is this a dagger which I see before me,
   The handle toward my hand? Come, let me clutch thee.
   I have thee not, and yet I see thee still.
   Art thou not, fatal vision, sensible   37
   To feeling as to sight? Or art thou but
   A dagger of the mind, a false creation,
   Proceeding from the heat-oppressèd brain?   40
   I see thee yet, in form as palpable
   As this which now I draw.   [*He draws a dagger.*]
   Thou marshall'st me the way that I was going,   43
   And such an instrument I was to use.

---

26 cleave . . . 'tis give me your support when the time comes   **27 So**
provided   **29 franchised** free (from guilt).   **clear** unstained
30 counseled receptive to suggestion   **32 drink** i.e., posset or bedtime
drink of hot spiced milk curdled with ale or wine, as also at 2.2.6
37 fatal ominous.   **sensible** perceivable by the senses   **40 heat-
oppressèd** fevered   **43 Thou . . . going** i.e., you seem to guide me toward
the destiny I intended, toward Duncan's chambers

Mine eyes are made the fools o' th' other senses,   45
Or else worth all the rest. I see thee still,   46
And on thy blade and dudgeon gouts of blood,   47
Which was not so before. There's no such thing.
It is the bloody business which informs   49
Thus to mine eyes. Now o'er the one half world
Nature seems dead, and wicked dreams abuse   51
The curtained sleep. Witchcraft celebrates   52
Pale Hecate's offerings, and withered Murder,   53
Alarumed by his sentinel, the wolf,   54
Whose howl's his watch, thus with his stealthy pace,   55
With Tarquin's ravishing strides, towards his design   56
Moves like a ghost. Thou sure and firm-set earth,
Hear not my steps which way they walk, for fear
Thy very stones prate of my whereabouts
And take the present horror from the time   60
Which now suits with it. Whiles I threat, he lives;   61
Words to the heat of deeds too cold breath gives.   62

                                        A bell rings.

I go, and it is done. The bell invites me.
Hear it not, Duncan, for it is a knell
That summons thee to heaven or to hell.   *Exit.*

2.2   *Enter Lady [Macbeth].*

LADY MACBETH
  That which hath made them drunk hath made me bold;

45–46 Mine . . . rest i.e., either this is a fantasy, deceiving me with what my eyes seem to see, or else it is a true vision expressing something that is beyond ordinary sensory experience   **47 dudgeon** hilt of a dagger.   **gouts** drops   **49 informs** creates forms or impressions   **51 abuse** deceive   **52 curtained** (1) veiled by bedcurtains (2) screened from rationality and consciousness   **53 Pale Hecate's offerings** sacrificial offerings to Hecate, the goddess of night and witchcraft. (She is *pale* because she is identified with the pale moon.)   **54 Alarumed** given the signal to action   **55 watch** i.e., watchword, or cry like the hourly call of the night watchman   **56 Tarquin's** (Tarquin was a Roman tyrant who ravished Lucrece.)   **60–61 And take . . . with it** and thus imitate and augment the horror which is so suited to this evil hour (?) or, remove the present horror, the murder, by crying out and revealing Macbeth's intent (?)   **62 Words . . . gives** i.e., words give only lifeless expression to live deeds, are no substitute for deeds

2.2. Location: Scene continues.

What hath quenched them hath given me fire. Hark!
  Peace!
It was the owl that shrieked, the fatal bellman,   3
Which gives the stern'st good-night. He is about it.   4
The doors are open; and the surfeited grooms   5
Do mock their charge with snores. I have drugged their
  possets,   6
That death and nature do contend about them
Whether they live or die.
MACBETH [*Within*]   Who's there? What, ho!
LADY MACBETH
  Alack, I am afraid they have awaked,
And 'tis not done. Th' attempt and not the deed
Confounds us. Hark! I laid their daggers ready;   11
He could not miss 'em. Had he not resembled
My father as he slept, I had done 't.

    Enter Macbeth, [*bearing bloody daggers*].

My husband!
MACBETH
  I have done the deed. Didst thou not hear a noise?
LADY MACBETH
  I heard the owl scream and the crickets cry.   16
Did not you speak?
MACBETH When?
LADY MACBETH Now.
MACBETH As I descended?
LADY MACBETH Ay.
MACBETH Hark! Who lies i' the second chamber?
LADY MACBETH Donalbain.
MACBETH This is a sorry sight. [*He looks at his hands.*]
LADY MACBETH
  A foolish thought, to say a sorry sight.
MACBETH
  There's one did laugh in 's sleep, and one cried
    "Murder!"

3 bellman one who rings a bell to announce a death or to mark the hours
of the night **4 stern'st good-night** i.e., notice to condemned criminals
that they are to be executed in the morning **5 grooms** servants
6 mock their charge make a mockery of their guard duty. **possets** hot
bedtime drinks, (as at 2.1.32) **11 Confounds** ruins **16 owl, crickets**
(The sounds of both could be ominous and prophetic of death.)

That they did wake each other. I stood and heard them.
But they did say their prayers, and addressed them   28-
Again to sleep.

LADY MACBETH   There are two lodged together.   29

MACBETH
One cried "God bless us!" and "Amen!" the other,
As they had seen me with these hangman's hands.   31
List'ning their fear, I could not say "Amen"
When they did say "God bless us!"

LADY MACBETH   Consider it not so deeply.

MACBETH
But wherefore could not I pronounce "Amen"?
I had most need of blessing, and "Amen"
Stuck in my throat.

LADY MACBETH   These deeds must not be thought   37
After these ways; so, it will make us mad.   38

MACBETH
Methought I heard a voice cry "Sleep no more!
Macbeth does murder sleep," the innocent sleep,
Sleep that knits up the raveled sleave of care,   41
The death of each day's life, sore labor's bath,   42
Balm of hurt minds, great nature's second course,   43
Chief nourisher in life's feast—

LADY MACBETH   What do you mean?

MACBETH
Still it cried "Sleep no more!" to all the house;
"Glamis hath murdered sleep, and therefore Cawdor
Shall sleep no more; Macbeth shall sleep no more."

LADY MACBETH
Who was it that thus cried? Why, worthy thane,
You do unbend your noble strength to think   49
So brainsickly of things. Go get some water
And wash this filthy witness from your hand.   51

---

28 addressed them settled themselves   **29 two** i.e., Malcolm and Donalbain   **31 As** as if.   **hangman's hands** bloody hands (because the hangman would draw and quarter the condemned, and also executed with an
ax)   **37 thought** thought about   **38 so** if we do so   **41 raveled sleave**
tangled skein   **42 bath** i.e., to relieve the soreness   **43 second course**
(Ordinary feasts had two courses, of which the second was the *chief
nourisher;* here, sleep is seen as following eating in a restorative pro-
cess.)   **49 unbend** slacken (as one would a bow; contrast "bend up" at
1.7.80)   **51 witness** evidence

Why did you bring these daggers from the place?
They must lie there. Go, carry them and smear
The sleepy grooms with blood.

MACBETH   I'll go no more.
I am afraid to think what I have done;
Look on 't again I dare not.

LADY MACBETH   Infirm of purpose!
Give me the daggers. The sleeping and the dead
Are but as pictures. 'Tis the eye of childhood
That fears a painted devil. If he do bleed,
I'll gild the faces of the grooms withal,   60
For it must seem their guilt.

                    [*She takes the daggers, and*] *exit.*
                                    Knock within.

MACBETH   Whence is that knocking?
How is 't with me, when every noise appalls me?
What hands are here? Ha! They pluck out mine eyes.
Will all great Neptune's ocean wash this blood
Clean from my hand? No, this my hand will rather
The multitudinous seas incarnadine,   66
Making the green one red.   67

          Enter Lady [*Macbeth*].

LADY MACBETH
My hands are of your color, but I shame
To wear a heart so white. (*Knock.*) I hear a knocking
At the south entry. Retire we to our chamber.
A little water clears us of this deed.
How easy is it, then! Your constancy   72
Hath left you unattended. (*Knock.*) Hark! More
  knocking.   73
Get on your nightgown, lest occasion call us   74
And show us to be watchers. Be not lost   75
So poorly in your thoughts.   76

---

60 gild (Gold was ordinarily spoken of as red.) **66 multitudinous**
existing in multitudes, numerous. **incarnadine** make red **67 one red**
one all-pervading red **72–73 Your . . . unattended** your firmness has
deserted you **74 nightgown** dressing gown **75 watchers** those who
have remained awake **76 poorly** dejectedly

MACBETH

To know my deed, 'twere best not know myself.   77

Knock.

Wake Duncan with thy knocking! I would thou
   couldst!   *Exeunt.*

2.3   *Knocking within. Enter a Porter.*

PORTER   Here's a knocking indeed! If a man were porter
of hell gate, he should have old turning the key. 2
(*Knock.*) Knock, knock, knock! Who's there, i' the
name of Beelzebub? Here's a farmer that hanged him- 4
self on th' expectation of plenty. Come in time! Have 5
napkins enough about you; here you'll sweat for 't. 6
(*Knock.*) Knock, knock! Who's there, in th' other
devil's name? Faith, here's an equivocator, that could 8
swear in both the scales against either scale, who committed treason enough for God's sake, yet could not
equivocate to heaven. O, come in, equivocator.
(*Knock.*) Knock, knock, knock! Who's there? Faith,
here's an English tailor come hither for stealing out of
a French hose. Come in, tailor. Here you may roast 14
your goose. (*Knock.*) Knock, knock! Never at quiet! 15

---

77 To . . . myself i.e., it were better to be lost in my thoughts than to
have consciousness of my deed; if I am to live with myself, I will have to
shut this out or be no longer the person I was

**2.3. Location: Scene continues. The knocking at the door has already
been heard in 2.2. It is not necessary to assume literally, however, that
Macbeth and Lady Macbeth have been talking near the** *south entry*
(2.2.70) where the knocking is heard.
2 old i.e., plenty of   **4–5 Here's . . . plenty** i.e., here's a farmer who
has hoarded in anticipation of a scarcity, and will be justly punished by a crop surplus and low prices   **5 Come in time** i.e., you have
come in good time   **6 napkins** handkerchiefs (to mop up the sweat)
8 equivocator (This is regarded by many editors as an allusion to the
trial of the Jesuit Henry Garnet for treason in the spring of 1606, and to
the doctrine of equivocation said to have been presented in his defense;
according to this doctrine a lie was not a lie if the utterer had in his
mind a different meaning in which the utterance was true.)   **14 French
hose** very narrow breeches and therefore hard for the tailor to steal
cloth from when he made them; or, very loose-fitting breeches, in which
case the tailor would easily be tempted to skimp on the cloth supplied
him for their manufacture   **14–15 roast your goose** heat your tailor's
smoothing iron (with an obvious pun)

What are you? But this place is too cold for hell. I'll
devil-porter it no further. I had thought to have let in
some of all professions that go the primrose way to th'
everlasting bonfire. (*Knock*.) Anon, anon! [*He opens
the gate*.] I pray you, remember the porter.

 Enter Macduff and Lennox.

MACDUFF
Was it so late, friend, ere you went to bed,
That you do lie so late?

PORTER Faith, sir, we were carousing till the second 23
cock; and drink, sir, is a great provoker of three things. 24

MACDUFF What three things does drink especially pro-
voke?

PORTER Marry, sir, nose-painting, sleep, and urine. 27
Lechery, sir, it provokes and unprovokes: it provokes
the desire but it takes away the performance. Therefore much drink may be said to be an equivocator
with lechery: it makes him and it mars him; it sets him
on and it takes him off; it persuades him and dis-
heartens him, makes him stand to and not stand to; 33
in conclusion, equivocates him in a sleep and, giving 34
him the lie, leaves him. 35

MACDUFF I believe drink gave thee the lie last night. 36

PORTER That it did, sir, i' the very throat on me. But I
requited him for his lie, and, I think, being too strong
for him, though he took up my legs sometimes, yet I 39
made a shift to cast him. 40

MACDUFF Is thy master stirring?

 Enter Macbeth.

Our knocking has awaked him. Here he comes.
         [*Exit Porter.*]

23–24 second cock i.e., 3 A.M., when the cock was thought to crow a
second time **27 Marry** (Originally, an oath, "by the Virgin Mary.")
nose-painting i.e., reddening of the nose through drink **33 makes . . .
stand to** stimulates him sexually but without sexual capability
34 equivocates . . . sleep (1) lulls him asleep (2) gives him an erotic
experience in dream only **34–35 giving him the lie** (1) deceiving him
(2) laying him out flat **35 leaves him** (1) dissipates as intoxication (2) is
passed off as urine **36 gave thee the lie** (1) called you a liar (2) made
you unable to stand, and put you to sleep **39 took up my legs** lifted me
as a wrestler would (with a suggestion of the drunkard's unsteadiness
on his legs, and perhaps also of lifting the leg as a dog might to urinate)
40 made a shift managed. **cast** (1) throw as in wrestling (2) vomit

LENNOX
  Good morrow, noble sir.
MACBETH   Good morrow, both.
MACDUFF
  Is the King stirring, worthy thane?
MACBETH   Not yet.
MACDUFF
  He did command me to call timely on him.   45
  I have almost slipped the hour.
MACBETH   I'll bring you to him.   46
MACDUFF
  I know this is a joyful trouble to you,
  But yet 'tis one.
MACBETH
  The labor we delight in physics pain.   49
  This is the door.
MACDUFF   I'll make so bold to call,
  For 'tis my limited service.   *Exit Macduff.* 51
LENNOX   Goes the King hence today?
MACBETH   He does; he did appoint so.
LENNOX
  The night has been unruly. Where we lay,
  Our chimneys were blown down, and, as they say,
  Lamentings heard i' th' air, strange screams of death,
  And prophesying with accents terrible   57
  Of dire combustion and confused events   58
  New hatched to the woeful time. The obscure bird   59
  Clamored the livelong night. Some say the earth
  Was feverous and did shake.
MACBETH   'Twas a rough night.
LENNOX
  My young remembrance cannot parallel
  A fellow to it.

      Enter Macduff.

MACDUFF   O, horror, horror, horror!
  Tongue nor heart cannot conceive nor name thee!

45 timely betimes, early   **46 slipped** let slip   **49 physics pain** i.e., cures
that labor of its troublesome aspect   **51 limited** appointed   **57 accents
terrible** terrifying utterances   **58 combustion** tumult   **59 New . . . time**
newly born to accompany the woeful nature of the time.   **obscure bird**
owl, the bird of darkness

MACBETH AND LENNOX   What's the matter?
MACDUFF
   Confusion now hath made his masterpiece!   66
   Most sacrilegious murder hath broke ope
   The Lord's anointed temple and stole thence
   The life o' the building!
MACBETH   What is 't you say? The life?
LENNOX   Mean you His Majesty?
MACDUFF
   Approach the chamber and destroy your sight
   With a new Gorgon. Do not bid me speak;   73
   See, and then speak yourselves.
                   Exeunt Macbeth and Lennox.
                    Awake, awake!
   Ring the alarum bell. Murder and treason!
   Banquo and Donalbain, Malcolm, awake!
   Shake off this downy sleep, death's counterfeit,
   And look on death itself! Up, up, and see
   The great doom's image! Malcolm, Banquo,   79
   As from your graves rise up and walk like sprites   80
   To countenance this horror! Ring the bell.   *Bell rings.*   81

     Enter Lady [Macbeth].

LADY MACBETH   What's the business,
   That such a hideous trumpet calls to parley   83
   The sleepers of the house? Speak, speak!
MACDUFF   O gentle lady,
   'Tis not for you to hear what I can speak.
   The repetition in a woman's ear   87
   Would murder as it fell.

     Enter Banquo.

               O Banquo, Banquo,
   Our royal master's murdered!

---

66 Confusion destruction   **73 Gorgon** one of three monsters with
hideous faces (Medusa was a Gorgon) whose look turned the beholders
to stone   **79 great doom's image** replica of Doomsday   **80 As . . . rise
up** (At the Last Judgment, the dead will rise from their graves to be
judged.)   **sprites** souls, ghosts   **81 countenance** (1) be in keeping with
(2) behold   **83 trumpet** (Another metaphorical suggestion of the Last
Judgment; the *trumpet* here is the shouting and the bell.)   **87 repetition** recital, report

LADY MACBETH   Woe, alas!
　What, in our house?
BANQUO   Too cruel anywhere.
　Dear Duff, I prithee, contradict thyself
　And say it is not so.

　　Enter Macbeth, Lennox, and Ross.

MACBETH
　Had I but died an hour before this chance   93
　I had lived a blessèd time; for from this instant
　There's nothing serious in mortality.   95
　All is but toys. Renown and grace is dead;   96
　The wine of life is drawn, and the mere lees   97
　Is left this vault to brag of.   98

　　Enter Malcolm and Donalbain.

DONALBAIN
　What is amiss?
MACBETH   You are, and do not know 't. 99
　The spring, the head, the fountain of your blood
　Is stopped, the very source of it is stopped.
MACDUFF
　Your royal father's murdered.
MALCOLM   O, by whom?
LENNOX
　Those of his chamber, as it seemed, had done 't.
　Their hands and faces were all badged with blood; 104
　So were their daggers, which unwiped we found
　Upon their pillows. They stared and were distracted;
　No man's life was to be trusted with them.
MACBETH
　O, yet I do repent me of my fury,
　That I did kill them.
MACDUFF   Wherefore did you so?
MACBETH
　Who can be wise, amazed, temp'rate and furious,   110
　Loyal and neutral, in a moment? No man.

---

93 chance occurrence (the murder of Duncan) **95 serious in mortality**
worthwhile in mortal life **96 toys** trifles **97 lees** dregs **98 vault** (1) wine-
vault (2) earth, with its vaulted sky **99 You are** i.e., you are amiss, having suffered the murder of your father **104 badged** marked as with a
badge or emblem **110 amazed** bewildered

Th' expedition of my violent love   112
Outrun the pauser, reason. Here lay Duncan,
His silver skin laced with his golden blood,   114
And his gashed stabs looked like a breach in nature   115
For ruin's wasteful entrance; there the murderers,   116
Steeped in the colors of their trade, their daggers
Unmannerly breeched with gore. Who could refrain   118
That had a heart to love, and in that heart
Courage to make 's love known?
LADY MACBETH [*Fainting*]   Help me hence, ho!   120
MACDUFF
  Look to the lady.
MALCOLM [*Aside to Donalbain*]
                    Why do we hold our tongues,
That most may claim this argument for ours?   122
DONALBAIN [*Aside to Malcolm*]
  What should be spoken here, where our fate,
Hid in an auger hole, may rush and seize us?   124
Let's away. Our tears are not yet brewed.
MALCOLM [*Aside to Donalbain*]
  Nor our strong sorrow upon the foot of motion.   126
BANQUO   Look to the lady.
                              [*Lady Macbeth is carried out.*]
And when we have our naked frailties hid,   128
That suffer in exposure, let us meet
And question this most bloody piece of work   130
To know it further. Fears and scruples shake us.   131
In the great hand of God I stand, and thence   132
Against the undivulged pretense I fight   133
Of treasonous malice.
MACDUFF   And so do I.
ALL   So all.   134

112 **expedition** haste   114 **golden** (See 2.2.60, note.)   115 **breach in
nature** gap in the defenses of life. (A metaphor of military siege.)
116 **wasteful** destructive   118 **breeched with gore** covered to the hilts
with gore (as with breeches)   120 **make 's love known** make manifest
his love   122 **argument** topic, business   124 **in an auger hole** i.e., in
some hiding place, in ambush   126 **upon . . . motion** yet in motion,
ready to act   128 **frailties hid** (1) bodies clothed (2) emotions con-
trolled   130 **question** discuss   131 **scruples** doubts, suspicions
132-134 **thence . . . malice** i.e., with God's help I will fight against the
as-yet-unknown purpose which prompted this treason   133 **pretense**
design   134 **malice** enmity

MACBETH
   Let's briefly put on manly readiness   135
   And meet i' the hall together.
ALL   Well contented.
        Exeunt [all but Malcolm and Donalbain].

MALCOLM
   What will you do? Let's not consort with them.   137
   To show an unfelt sorrow is an office
   Which the false man does easy. I'll to England.   139

DONALBAIN
   To Ireland, I. Our separated fortune
   Shall keep us both the safer. Where we are,
   There's daggers in men's smiles; the nea'er in blood,   142
   The nearer bloody.
MALCOLM   This murderous shaft that's shot   143
   Hath not yet lighted, and our safest way   144
   Is to avoid the aim. Therefore to horse,
   And let us not be dainty of leave-taking,   146
   But shift away. There's warrant in that theft   147
   Which steals itself when there's no mercy left.
                      Exeunt.

❖

2.4   *Enter Ross with an Old Man.*

OLD MAN
   Threescore and ten I can remember well,
   Within the volume of which time I have seen
   Hours dreadful and things strange, but this sore night   3
   Hath trifled former knowings.
ROSS   Ha, good father,   4
   Thou seest the heavens, as troubled with man's act,   5
   Threatens his bloody stage. By th' clock 'tis day,   6

---

135 briefly quickly.   **manly readiness** men's clothing, or armor
137 consort keep company, associate   **139 easy** easily   **142 nea'er**
nearer   **143 The nearer bloody** i.e., the greater the danger of being
murdered   **144 lighted** alighted, descended   **146 dainty of** particular
about   **147 shift away** disappear by stealth.   **warrant** justification

2.4. Location: Outside Macbeth's castle of Inverness.
3 sore dreadful, grievous   **4 trifled former knowings** made trivial all
former experiences.   **father** old man   **5-6 heavens, act, stage** (A theatrical metaphor; the *heavens* are the decorated roof over the *stage*.)

And yet dark night strangles the traveling lamp.   7
Is 't night's predominance or the day's shame   8
That darkness does the face of earth entomb
When living light should kiss it?
OLD MAN   'Tis unnatural,
Even like the deed that's done. On Tuesday last
A falcon, towering in her pride of place,   12
Was by a mousing owl hawked at and killed.   13
ROSS
And Duncan's horses—a thing most strange and
    certain—
Beauteous and swift, the minions of their race,   15
Turned wild in nature, broke their stalls, flung out,
Contending 'gainst obedience, as they would   17
Make war with mankind.
OLD MAN   'Tis said they eat each other. 18
ROSS
They did so, to th' amazement of mine eyes
That looked upon 't.

        Enter Macduff.

                          Here comes the good Macduff.—
How goes the world, sir, now?
MACDUFF   Why, see you not?
ROSS
Is 't known who did this more than bloody deed?
MACDUFF
Those that Macbeth hath slain.
ROSS   Alas the day,
What good could they pretend?
MACDUFF   They were suborned.   24
Malcolm and Donalbain, the King's two sons,
Are stolen away and fled, which puts upon them
Suspicion of the deed.
ROSS   'Gainst nature still!

---

7 traveling lamp i.e., sun **8 predominance** ascendancy, superior influence (as of a heavenly body) **12 towering** circling higher and higher. (A
term in falconry.) **place** pitch, highest point in the falcon's flight
13 mousing i.e., ordinarily preying on mice **15 minions** darlings **17 as**
as if **18 eat** ate. (Pronounced "et.") **24 What . . . pretend** i.e., what
could they hope to gain by it. **pretend** intend. **suborned** bribed, hired

Thriftless ambition, that will ravin up   28
Thine own life's means! Then 'tis most like
The sovereignty will fall upon Macbeth.

MACDUFF
He is already named and gone to Scone   31
To be invested.

ROSS   Where is Duncan's body?

MACDUFF   Carried to Colmekill,   33
The sacred storehouse of his predecessors
And guardian of their bones.

ROSS   Will you to Scone?

MACDUFF
No, cousin, I'll to Fife.

ROSS   Well, I will thither.   36

MACDUFF
Well, may you see things well done there. Adieu,
Lest our old robes sit easier than our new!

ROSS   Farewell, father.

OLD MAN
God's benison go with you, and with those   40
That would make good of bad, and friends of foes!

                              Exeunt omnes.

❖

28 Thriftless wasteful.   **ravin up** devour ravenously   **31 named** chosen.
(See 1.4.50, note.)   **Scone** ancient royal city of Scotland near Perth
33 Colmekill Icolmkill, i.e., Cell of St. Columba, the barren islet of Iona
in the Western Islands, a sacred spot where the kings were buried; here
called a *storehouse*   **36 Fife** (Of which Macduff is Thane.)   **40 benison**
blessing

3.1   *Enter Banquo.*

BANQUO
 Thou hast it now—King, Cawdor, Glamis, all
 As the weird women promised, and I fear
 Thou played'st most foully for 't. Yet it was said
 It should not stand in thy posterity,   4
 But that myself should be the root and father
 Of many kings. If there come truth from them—
 As upon thee, Macbeth, their speeches shine—   7
 Why, by the verities on thee made good,
 May they not be my oracles as well
 And set me up in hope? But hush, no more.   10

 *Sennet sounded. Enter Macbeth as King, Lady
 [Macbeth], Lennox, Ross, lords, and attendants.*

MACBETH
 Here's our chief guest.
LADY MACBETH   · If he had been forgotten,
 It had been as a gap in our great feast
 And all-thing unbecoming.   13
MACBETH
 Tonight we hold a solemn supper, sir,   14
 And I'll request your presence.
BANQUO   Let Your Highness
 Command upon me, to the which my duties   16
 Are with a most indissoluble tie
 Forever knit.
MACBETH   Ride you this afternoon?
BANQUO   Ay, my good lord.
MACBETH
 We should have else desired your good advice,
 Which still hath been both grave and prosperous,   22
 In this day's council; but we'll take tomorrow.
 Is 't far you ride?

3.1. Location: Forres. The palace.
4 stand stay, remain   **7 shine** are brilliantly manifest   **10 s.d. Sennet**
trumpet call   **13 all-thing** in every way   **14 solemn** ceremonious
16 Command lay your command   **22 still** always.   **grave** weighty.
prosperous profitable

BANQUO
  As far, my lord, as will fill up the time
  Twixt this and supper. Go not my horse the better,   26
  I must become a borrower of the night
  For a dark hour or twain.
MACBETH   Fail not our feast.
BANQUO   My lord, I will not.
MACBETH
  We hear our bloody cousins are bestowed   31
  In England and in Ireland, not confessing
  Their cruel parricide, filling their hearers
  With strange invention. But of that tomorrow,   34
  When therewithal we shall have cause of state   35
  Craving us jointly. Hie you to horse. Adieu,   36
  Till you return at night. Goes Fleance with you?
BANQUO
  Ay, my good lord. Our time does call upon 's.
MACBETH
  I wish your horses swift and sure of foot,
  And so I do commend you to their backs.   40
  Farewell.   *Exit Banquo.*
  Let every man be master of his time
  Till seven at night. To make society
  The sweeter welcome, we will keep ourself   44
  Till suppertime alone. While then, God be with you!   45
            Exeunt Lords [and all but Macbeth
                          and a Servant.]
  Sirrah, a word with you. Attend those men   46
  Our pleasure?
SERVANT
  They are, my lord, without the palace gate.
MACBETH
  Bring them before us.   *Exit Servant.*
                To be thus is nothing,   49
  But to be safely thus.—Our fears in Banquo   50

---

26 Go . . . better i.e., unless my horse makes better time than I expect
31 bestowed lodged   **34 invention** falsehood (i.e., that Macbeth was the
murderer)   **35 therewithal** besides that   **35–36 cause . . . jointly** questions
of state occupying our joint attention   **40 commend** commit, entrust
44 keep ourself keep to myself   **45 While** till   **46 Sirrah** (A form of address to a social inferior.)   **49 thus** i.e., king   **50 But** unless.   **in** concerning

Stick deep, and in his royalty of nature   51
Reigns that which would be feared. 'Tis much he dares;   52
And to that dauntless temper of his mind   53
He hath a wisdom that doth guide his valor
To act in safety. There is none but he
Whose being I do fear; and under him
My genius is rebuked, as it is said   57
Mark Antony's was by Caesar. He chid the sisters   58
When first they put the name of king upon me,
And bade them speak to him. Then, prophetlike,
They hailed him father to a line of kings.
Upon my head they placed a fruitless crown
And put a barren scepter in my grip
Thence to be wrenched with an unlineal hand,   64
No son of mine succeeding. If 't be so,
For Banquo's issue have I filed my mind;   66
For them the gracious Duncan have I murdered,
Put rancors in the vessel of my peace   68
Only for them, and mine eternal jewel   69
Given to the common enemy of man   70
To make them kings, the seeds of Banquo kings.
Rather than so, come fate into the list,   72
And champion me to th' utterance!—Who's there?   73

Enter Servant and two Murderers.

Now go to the door, and stay there till we call.
                                             Exit Servant.
Was it not yesterday we spoke together?
MURDERERS
It was, so please Your Highness.
MACBETH   Well then, now
Have you considered of my speeches? Know
That it was he in the times past which held you

---

51 royalty of nature natural kingly bearing   **52 would be** deserves
to be   **53 to** added to   **57 genius** guardian spirit.   **rebuked** abashed,
daunted   **58 Caesar** Octavius Caesar   **64 with** by.   **unlineal** not of
lineal descent from me   **66 filed** defiled   **68 rancors** malignant enemies (here visualized as a poison added to a vessel full of wholesome drink)   **69 eternal jewel** i.e., soul   **70 common . . . man** i.e.,
devil   **72 list** lists, place of combat   **73 champion me** fight with me
in single combat.   **to th' utterance** to the last extremity (French, *à
l'outrance*)

So under fortune, which you thought had been   79
Our innocent self. This I made good to you
In our last conference, passed in probation with you   81
How you were borne in hand, how crossed, the
   instruments,   82
Who wrought with them, and all things else that might
To half a soul and to a notion crazed   84
Say, "Thus did Banquo."

FIRST MURDERER   You made it known to us.

MACBETH
I did so, and went further, which is now
Our point of second meeting. Do you find
Your patience so predominant in your nature
That you can let this go? Are you so gospeled   89
To pray for this good man and for his issue,
Whose heavy hand hath bowed you to the grave
And beggared yours forever?

FIRST MURDERER   We are men, my liege.   92

MACBETH
Ay, in the catalogue ye go for men,   93
As hounds and greyhounds, mongrels, spaniels, curs,
Shoughs, water-rugs, and demi-wolves are clept   95
All by the name of dogs. The valued file   96
Distinguishes the swift, the slow, the subtle,
The housekeeper, the hunter, every one   98
According to the gift which bounteous nature
Hath in him closed, whereby he does receive   100
Particular addition from the bill   101
That writes them all alike; and so of men.   102
Now, if you have a station in the file,   103
Not i' the worst rank of manhood, say 't,
And I will put that business in your bosoms

---

79 under out of favor with   **81 passed in probation** went over the proof   **82 borne in hand** deceived by false promises. **crossed** thwarted. **instruments** agents   **84 To half a soul** even to a half-wit. **notion** mind   **89 gospeled** imbued with the gospel spirit   **92 yours** your family   **93 go for** pass for, are entered for   **95 Shoughs** a kind of shaggy dog. **water-rugs** long-haired water dogs. **demi-wolves** a cross-breed with the wolf. **clept** called   **96 valued file** list classified according to value   **98 housekeeper** watchdog   **100 in him closed** enclosed in him, set in him like a jewel   **101–102 Particular . . . alike** particular qualification apart from the catalog that lists them all indiscriminately   **103 file** military row, as in "rank and file"; see *rank* in l. 104

Whose execution takes your enemy off,
Grapples you to the heart and love of us,
Who wear our health but sickly in his life,   108
Which in his death were perfect.
SECOND MURDERER   I am one, my liege,
Whom the vile blows and buffets of the world
Hath so incensed that I am reckless what
I do to spite the world.
FIRST MURDERER   And I another,
So weary with disasters, tugged with fortune,   113
That I would set my life on any chance   114
To mend it or be rid on 't.
MACBETH   Both of you
Know Banquo was your enemy.
BOTH MURDERERS   True, my lord.
MACBETH
So is he mine, and in such bloody distance   117
That every minute of his being thrusts   118
Against my near'st of life. And though I could   119
With barefaced power sweep him from my sight   120
And bid my will avouch it, yet I must not,   121
For certain friends that are both his and mine,   122
Whose loves I may not drop, but wail his fall   123
Who I myself struck down. And thence it is   124
That I to your assistance do make love,   125
Masking the business from the common eye
For sundry weighty reasons.
SECOND MURDERER   We shall, my lord,
Perform what you command us.
FIRST MURDERER   Though our lives—
MACBETH
Your spirits shine through you. Within this hour at most   129
I will advise you where to plant yourselves,   130

---

108 in his life while he lives   **113 tugged with** pulled about by (as in
wrestling)   **114 set** risk, stake   **117 distance** (1) hostility, enmity
(2) interval of distance to be kept between fencers   **118 thrusts** (as in
fencing)   **119 near'st of life** most vital part, the heart   **120 With barefaced power** by open use of my supreme royal authority   **121 And . . .
avouch it** and use my mere wish as my justification   **122 For** because
of, for the sake of   **123 wail** i.e., I must lament   **124 Who** he whom
125 to . . . make love woo your aid   **129 Your . . . you** i.e., enough; I can
see your determination in your faces   **130 advise** instruct

Acquaint you with the perfect spy o' the time, 131
The moment on 't, for 't must be done tonight,
And something from the palace; always thought 133
That I require a clearness. And with him— 134
To leave no rubs nor botches in the work— 135
Fleance his son, that keeps him company,
Whose absence is no less material to me
Than is his father's, must embrace the fate
Of that dark hour. Resolve yourselves apart; 139
I'll come to you anon.
BOTH MURDERERS   We are resolved, my lord.
MACBETH
I'll call upon you straight. Abide within.
Exeunt [*Murderers*].
It is concluded. Banquo, thy soul's flight,
If it find heaven, must find it out tonight.   [*Exit.*]

❖

3.2   *Enter Macbeth's Lady and a Servant.*

LADY MACBETH   Is Banquo gone from court?
SERVANT
Ay, madam, but returns again tonight.
LADY MACBETH
Say to the King I would attend his leisure
For a few words.
SERVANT   Madam, I will.   *Exit.*
LADY MACBETH   Naught's had, all's spent,
Where our desire is got without content. 7
'Tis safer to be that which we destroy
Than by destruction dwell in doubtful joy. 9

   Enter Macbeth.

How now, my lord? Why do you keep alone,

---

131 perfect spy o' the time knowledge or espial of the exact time (?)
133 something from some distance removed from.   **thought** being
borne in mind   **134 clearness** freedom from suspicion   **135 rubs** de-
fects, rough spots   **139 Resolve yourselves apart** make up your minds
in private conference

3.2. Location: The palace.
7 content contentedness   **9 Than . . . joy** than by destroying achieve
only an apprehensive joy

Of sorriest fancies your companions making, 11
Using those thoughts which should indeed have died 12
With them they think on? Things without all remedy 13
Should be without regard. What's done is done. 14

MACBETH
We have scorched the snake, not killed it. 15
She'll close and be herself, whilst our poor malice 16
Remains in danger of her former tooth. 17
But let the frame of things disjoint, both the worlds
    suffer, 18
Ere we will eat our meal in fear and sleep
In the affliction of these terrible dreams
That shake us nightly. Better be with the dead,
Whom we, to gain our peace, have sent to peace, 22
Than on the torture of the mind to lie 23
In restless ecstasy. Duncan is in his grave; 24
After life's fitful fever he sleeps well. 25
Treason has done his worst; nor steel, nor poison,
Malice domestic, foreign levy, nothing 27
Can touch him further.

LADY MACBETH   Come on,
Gentle my lord, sleek o'er your rugged looks. 30
Be bright and jovial among your guests tonight.

MACBETH
So shall I, love, and so, I pray, be you.
Let your remembrance apply to Banquo; 33
Present him eminence, both with eye and tongue— 34
Unsafe the while, that we 35
Must lave our honors in these flattering streams 36

11 **sorriest** most despicable or wretched   12 **Using** keeping company
with, entertaining   13 **without** beyond   14 **without regard** not pon-
dered upon   15 **scorched** slashed, cut   16 **close** heal, close up again.
poor malice feeble hostility   17 **her former tooth** her fang, just as
before   18 **let . . . suffer** let the universe itself fall apart, both heaven
and earth perish   22 **to gain . . . peace** to gain contentedness through
satisfaction of desire, have sent to their eternal rest   23 **torture** rack
24 **ecstasy** frenzy   25 **fitful** characterized by paroxysms; or, intermit-
tent   27 **Malice domestic** civil war.   **foreign levy** levying of troops
abroad (against Scotland)   30 **Gentle . . . looks** my noble lord, smooth
over your rough looks   33 **remembrance** greetings expressive of remembrance.   **apply** be shown   34 **eminence** favor   35–36 **Unsafe . . .
streams** i.e., we are unsafe at present, and so must put on a show of
flattering cordiality to make our reputation look clean; or, we are unsafe
so long as we must flatter thus. (*Lave* means "wash.")

And make our faces vizards to our hearts,   37
Disguising what they are.
LADY MACBETH   You must leave this.
MACBETH
O, full of scorpions is my mind, dear wife!
Thou know'st that Banquo and his Fleance lives.
LADY MACBETH
But in them nature's copy's not eterne.   41
MACBETH
There's comfort yet; they are assailable.   42
Then be thou jocund. Ere the bat hath flown
His cloistered flight, ere to black Hecate's summons   44
The shard-borne beetle with his drowsy hums   45
Hath rung night's yawning peal, there shall be done   46
A deed of dreadful note.
LADY MACBETH   What's to be done?
MACBETH
Be innocent of the knowledge, dearest chuck,   48
Till thou applaud the deed. Come, seeling night,   49
Scarf up the tender eye of pitiful day,   50
And with thy bloody and invisible hand
Cancel and tear to pieces that great bond   52
Which keeps me pale! Light thickens,   53
And the crow makes wing to the rooky wood;   54
Good things of day begin to droop and drowse,
Whiles night's black agents to their preys do rouse.   56
Thou marvel'st at my words, but hold thee still.
Things bad begun make strong themselves by ill.
So, prithee, go with me.   *Exeunt.*

❖

37 vizards masks   **41 nature's copy** lease of life (i.e., by copyhold or lease subject to cancellation); also, the individual man made from nature's mold.   **eterne** perpetual   **42 There's** i.e., in that thought there is   **44 cloistered** i.e., in and among buildings   **45 shard-borne** borne on shards, or horny wing cases; or, *shard-born,* bred in cow-droppings (shards)   **46 yawning** drowsy   **48 chuck** (A term of endearment.)   **49 seeling** eye-closing. (Night is pictured here as a falconer sewing up the eyes of day lest it should struggle against the deed that is to be done.)   **50 Scarf up** blindfold.   **pitiful** compassionate   **52 bond** i.e., Banquo's lease of life   **53 pale** pallid from fear (with a suggestion perhaps of *paled,* fenced in).   **thickens** grows opaque and dim   **54 crow** rook.   **rooky** full of rooks   **56 to . . . rouse** bestir themselves to hunt their prey

3.3 *Enter three Murderers.*

FIRST MURDERER
  But who did bid thee join with us?
THIRD MURDERER   Macbeth.
SECOND MURDERER [*To the First Murderer*]
  He needs not our mistrust, since he delivers   2
  Our offices and what we have to do   3
  To the direction just.
FIRST MURDERER   Then stand with us.   4
  The west yet glimmers with some streaks of day.
  Now spurs the lated traveler apace   6
  To gain the timely inn, and near approaches   7
  The subject of our watch.
THIRD MURDERER   Hark, I hear horses.
BANQUO (*Within*) Give us a light there, ho!
SECOND MURDERER   Then 'tis he. The rest
  That are within the note of expectation   12
  Already are i' the court.
FIRST MURDERER   His horses go about.
THIRD MURDERER
  Almost a mile; but he does usually—
  So all men do—from hence to the palace gate
  Make it their walk.

          Enter Banquo and Fleance, with a torch.

SECOND MURDERER   A light, a light!
THIRD MURDERER   'Tis he.
FIRST MURDERER   Stand to 't.
BANQUO   It will be rain tonight.
FIRST MURDERER   Let it come down!
                              [*They attack Banquo.*]
BANQUO
  O, treachery! Fly, good Fleance, fly, fly, fly!
  Thou mayst revenge.—O slave!
                              [*He dies. Fleance escapes.*]

3.3. Location: A park near the palace.
2–3 He . . . offices we need not mistrust this man, since he states exactly our duties (as told us by Macbeth)   **4 To** according to.   **just**
exactly. (That is, one can tell he comes from Macbeth, since he has
identical instructions.)   **6 lated** belated   **7 timely** arrived at in good
time   **12 note of expectation** list of those expected

THIRD MURDERER
  Who did strike out the light?

FIRST MURDERER   Was 't not the way?   25

THIRD MURDERER
  There's but one down; the son is fled.

SECOND MURDERER
  We have lost best half of our affair.

FIRST MURDERER
  Well, let's away and say how much is done.   28

                        Exeunt.

❖

3.4   *Banquet prepared. Enter Macbeth, Lady*
        [Macbeth], Ross, Lennox, Lords, and
        attendants.

MACBETH
  You know your own degrees; sit down. At first   1
  And last, the hearty welcome.   *[They sit.]*

LORDS   Thanks to Your Majesty.   2

MACBETH
  Ourself will mingle with society   3
  And play the humble host.
  Our hostess keeps her state, but in best time   5
  We will require her welcome.   6

LADY MACBETH
  Pronounce it for me, sir, to all our friends,
  For my heart speaks they are welcome.

   Enter First Murderer [to the door].

MACBETH
  See, they encounter thee with their hearts' thanks.   9
  Both sides are even. Here I'll sit i' the midst.   10

---

25 way i.e., thing to do   **28 s.d. Exeunt** (Presumably the murderers drag the body of Banquo offstage as they go.)

3.4. Location: A room of state in the palace.
1 degrees ranks (as a determinant of seating)   **1–2 At . . . last** once for all   **3 mingle with society** i.e., leave the chair of state and circulate among the guests   **5 keeps her state** remains in her canopied chair of state.   **in best time** when it is most appropriate   **6 require** request **9 encounter** respond to   **10 even** full, with equal numbers on both sides

Be large in mirth; anon we'll drink a measure   11
The table round. [*He goes to the Murderer.*]
   There's blood upon thy face.

MURDERER   'Tis Banquo's then.

MACBETH
'Tis better thee without than he within.   14
Is he dispatched?

MURDERER
My lord, his throat is cut. That I did for him.

MACBETH   Thou art the best o' the cutthroats.
Yet he's good that did the like for Fleance;
If thou didst it, thou art the nonpareil.   19

MURDERER   Most royal sir, Fleance is scaped.

MACBETH
Then comes my fit again. I had else been perfect,
Whole as the marble, founded as the rock,   22
As broad and general as the casing air.   23
But now I am cabined, cribbed, confined, bound in   24
To saucy doubts and fears. But Banquo's safe?   25

MURDERER
Ay, my good lord. Safe in a ditch he bides,
With twenty trenchèd gashes on his head,
The least a death to nature.

MACBETH   Thanks for that.
There the grown serpent lies; the worm that's fled   29
Hath nature that in time will venom breed,
No teeth for the present. Get thee gone. Tomorrow
We'll hear ourselves again.   *Exit Murderer.*

LADY MACBETH   My royal lord,   32
You do not give the cheer. The feast is sold   33
That is not often vouched, while 'tis a-making,   34
'Tis given with welcome. To feed were best at home;   35

---

11 large liberal, free. **measure** bumper **14 'Tis ... within** it is better
for you to have it on you than he to have it within him **19 the nonpareil** without equal **22 founded** firmly established **23 broad and
general** unconfined. **casing** encasing, enveloping **24 cribbed** shut in
25 saucy sharp, impudent, importunate **29 worm** small serpent
32 hear ourselves confer **33–35 is sold ... welcome** i.e., seems grudg-
ingly given, as if in return for money, unless it is often accompanied
with assurances of welcome while it is in progress **35 To feed ...
home** i.e., mere eating is best done at home

From thence, the sauce to meat is ceremony;   36
Meeting were bare without it.   37

     Enter the Ghost of Banquo, and sits in Macbeth's
     place.

MACBETH   Sweet remembrancer!
Now, good digestion wait on appetite,   38
And health on both!

LENNOX   May 't please Your Highness sit?

MACBETH
Here had we now our country's honor roofed   40
Were the graced person of our Banquo present,   41
Who may I rather challenge for unkindness   42
Than pity for mischance.

ROSS   His absence, sir,
Lays blame upon his promise. Please 't Your Highness
To grace us with your royal company?

MACBETH [*Seeing his place occupied*]
The table's full.

LENNOX   Here is a place reserved, sir.

MACBETH Where?

LENNOX
Here, my good lord. What is 't that moves Your
   Highness?

MACBETH
Which of you have done this?

LORDS   What, my good lord?

MACBETH
Thou canst not say I did it. Never shake
Thy gory locks at me.

ROSS
Gentlemen, rise. His Highness is not well.
                [They start to rise.]

LADY MACBETH
Sit, worthy friends. My lord is often thus,
And hath been from his youth. Pray you, keep seat.

---

36 From thence i.e., away from home, dining in company. **meat** food
37 Meeting were bare gatherings of friends would be unadorned
38 wait on attend **40 roofed** under one roof **41 graced** gracious
42 Who may I whom I hope I may. **challenge for** reprove for

The fit is momentary; upon a thought   55
He will again be well. If much you note him
You shall offend him and extend his passion.   57
Feed, and regard him not.—[*She confers apart with*
    Macbeth.] Are you a man?

MACBETH
Ay, and a bold one, that dare look on that
Which might appall the devil.

LADY MACBETH   O, proper stuff!   60
This is the very painting of your fear.
This is the air-drawn dagger which, you said,   62
Led you to Duncan. O, these flaws and starts,   63
Impostors to true fear, would well become   64
A woman's story at a winter's fire,
Authorized by her grandam. Shame itself!   66
Why do you make such faces? When all's done,
You look but on a stool.

MACBETH   Prithee, see there!
Behold, look! Lo, how say you?
Why, what care I? If thou canst nod, speak too.
If charnel houses and our graves must send   71
Those that we bury back, our monuments   72
Shall be the maws of kites.   [*Exit Ghost*.]   73

LADY MACBETH   What, quite unmanned in folly?

MACBETH
If I stand here, I saw him.

LADY MACBETH   Fie, for shame!

MACBETH
Blood hath been shed ere now, i' th' olden time,
Ere humane statute purged the gentle weal;   77
Ay, and since too, murders have been performed
Too terrible for the ear. The time has been
That, when the brains were out, the man would die,

55 **upon a thought** in a moment   57 **offend him** make him worse.
extend prolong   60 **O, proper stuff** O, nonsense   62 **air-drawn** made of
thin air, or floating disembodied in space   63 **flaws** gusts, outbursts
64 **to** compared with.   **become** befit   66 **Authorized** told on the authority of   71 **charnel houses** depositories for bones or bodies   72–73 **our**
. . . kites i.e., we will have to leave the unburied bodies to scavenging
birds of prey   77 **Ere . . . weal** before the institution of law cleansed the
commonwealth of violence and made it gentle.   **humane** (This spelling,
interchangeable with *human*, carries both meanings: "appertaining to
humankind" and "befitting humanity.")

And there an end; but now they rise again
With twenty mortal murders on their crowns,   82
And push us from our stools. This is more strange   83
Than such a murder is.

LADY MACBETH   My worthy lord,
Your noble friends do lack you.

MACBETH   I do forget.
Do not muse at me, my most worthy friends;
I have a strange infirmity, which is nothing
To those that know me. Come, love and health to all!
Then I'll sit down. Give me some wine. Fill full.
                              [*He is given wine.*]

    Enter Ghost.

I drink to the general joy o' the whole table,
And to our dear friend Banquo, whom we miss.
Would he were here! To all, and him, we thirst,   92
And all to all.

LORDS   Our duties and the pledge.   93
                              [*They drink.*]

MACBETH [*Seeing the Ghost*]
Avaunt, and quit my sight! Let the earth hide thee!
Thy bones are marrowless, thy blood is cold;
Thou hast no speculation in those eyes   96
Which thou dost glare with.

LADY MACBETH   Think of this, good peers,
But as a thing of custom. 'Tis no other;
Only it spoils the pleasure of the time.

MACBETH   What man dare, I dare.
Approach thou like the rugged Russian bear,   101
The armed rhinoceros, or the Hyrcan tiger;   102
Take any shape but that, and my firm nerves   103
Shall never tremble. Or be alive again
And dare me to the desert with thy sword.   105

---

82 mortal murders deadly wounds. **crowns** heads **83 push . . . stools**
usurp our places at feasts (with a suggestion of usurpation of the
throne) **92 thirst** desire to drink **93 all to all** all good wishes to all; or,
let all drink to everyone else. **Our . . . pledge** in drinking the toast you
just proposed, we offer our homage **96 speculation** power of sight
101 like in the likeness of **102 armed** armor-plated. **Hyrcan** of Hyrca-
nia, in ancient times a region near the Caspian Sea **103 nerves** sinews
105 the desert some solitary place

If trembling I inhabit then, protest me   106
The baby of a girl. Hence, horrible shadow!   107
Unreal mockery, hence! [*Exit Ghost.*] Why, so; being
      gone,
I am a man again. Pray you, sit still.

LADY MACBETH
You have displaced the mirth, broke the good meeting
With most admired disorder.

MACBETH   Can such things be,   111
And overcome us like a summer's cloud,   112
Without our special wonder? You make me strange   113
Even to the disposition that I owe,   114
When now I think you can behold such sights
And keep the natural ruby of your cheeks
When mine is blanched with fear.

ROSS   What sights, my lord?

LADY MACBETH
I pray you, speak not. He grows worse and worse;
Question enrages him. At once, good night.   119
Stand not upon the order of your going,   120
But go at once.

LENNOX   Good night, and better health   121
Attend His Majesty!

LADY MACBETH   A kind good night to all!
                    Exeunt Lords [and attendants].

MACBETH
It will have blood, they say; blood will have blood.
Stones have been known to move, and trees to speak;   124
Augurs and understood relations have   125
By maggotpies and choughs and rooks brought forth   126
The secret'st man of blood. What is the night?   127

---

106 If . . . then i.e., if then I tremble. **protest** proclaim   **107 The baby
of a girl** a baby girl, or, girl's doll   **111 admired** wondered at.   **disorder**
lack of self-control   **112 overcome** come over   **113–114 You make . . .
owe** you cause me to feel I do not know my own nature (which I had
presumed to be that of a brave man)   **119 Question** talk.   **At once** to
you all; now   **120 Stand . . . going** i.e., do not take the time to leave in
ceremonious order of rank, as you entered   **121 at once** all together and
now   **124 Stones . . . speak** i.e., even inanimate nature speaks in such a
way as to reveal the unnatural act of murder   **125 Augurs** auguries.
understood relations comprehended reports or utterances   **126 By . . .
choughs** by means of magpies and jackdaws.   **brought forth** revealed
127 man of blood murderer.   **the night** i.e., the time of night

LADY MACBETH
　Almost at odds with morning, which is which.

MACBETH
　How sayst thou, that Macduff denies his person　　　129
　At our great bidding?

LADY MACBETH　　　　　　　Did you send to him, sir?

MACBETH
　I hear it by the way; but I will send.　　　　　　131
　There's not a one of them but in his house
　I keep a servant fee'd. I will tomorrow—　　　　133
　And betimes I will—to the Weird Sisters.　　　　134
　More shall they speak, for now I am bent to know　135
　By the worst means the worst. For mine own good
　All causes shall give way. I am in blood　　　　137
　Stepped in so far that, should I wade no more,　　138
　Returning were as tedious as go o'er.　　　　　139
　Strange things I have in head, that will to hand,
　Which must be acted ere they may be scanned.　　141

LADY MACBETH
　You lack the season of all natures, sleep.　　　142

MACBETH
　Come, we'll to sleep. My strange and self-abuse　143
　Is the initiate fear that wants hard use.　　　144
　We are yet but young in deed.　　　　　　*Exeunt.*

❖

3.5　　*Thunder. Enter the three Witches,*
　　　　　meeting Hecate.

FIRST WITCH
　Why, how now, Hecate? You look angerly.　　　　1

129 How sayst thou what do you say to the fact that　**131 by the way**
indirectly　**133 fee'd** i.e., paid to spy　**134 betimes** (1) early (2) while
there is still time　**135 bent** determined　**137 All causes** all other
considerations　**138 should . . . more** even if I were to wade no farther　**139 were** would be.　**go** going　**141 ere . . . scanned** i.e., even
before thinking about them carefully, at once　**142 season** preserva-
tive　**143 strange and self-abuse** strange self-delusion　**144 initiate
fear** fear experienced by a novice.　**wants hard use** lacks toughening experience

3.5. Location: A heath. (This scene is probably by another author.)
1 angerly angrily, angry

HECATE
> Have I not reason, beldams as you are?   2
> Saucy and overbold, how did you dare
> To trade and traffic with Macbeth
> In riddles and affairs of death,
> And I, the mistress of your charms,
> The close contriver of all harms,   7
> Was never called to bear my part
> Or show the glory of our art?
> And, which is worse, all you have done
> Hath been but for a wayward son,
> Spiteful and wrathful, who, as others do,
> Loves for his own ends, not for you.
> But make amends now. Get you gone,
> And at the pit of Acheron   15
> Meet me i' the morning. Thither he
> Will come to know his destiny.
> Your vessels and your spells provide,
> Your charms and everything beside.
> I am for th' air. This night I'll spend
> Unto a dismal and a fatal end.   21
> Great business must be wrought ere noon.
> Upon the corner of the moon
> There hangs a vaporous drop profound;   24
> I'll catch it ere it come to ground,
> And that, distilled by magic sleights,
> Shall raise such artificial sprites   27
> As by the strength of their illusion
> Shall draw him on to his confusion   29
> He shall spurn fate, scorn death, and bear
> His hopes 'bove wisdom, grace, and fear.
> And you all know, security   32
> Is mortals' chiefest enemy.   *Music and a song.*
> Hark! I am called. My little spirit, see,
> Sits in a foggy cloud and stays for me.   [*Exit.*] 35
>   *Sing within,* "Come away, come away," *etc.*

2 **beldams** hags   7 **close** secret   15 **Acheron** the river of sorrows in Hades; here, hell itself   21 **dismal** disastrous, ill-omened   24 **profound** i.e., heavily pendent, ready to drop off   27 **artificial** produced by magical arts   29 **confusion** ruin   32 **security** overconfidence   35 **s.d. Come away** etc. (The song occurs in Thomas Middleton's *The Witch*.)

FIRST WITCH
    Come, let's make haste. She'll soon be back again.
                               Exeunt.

❖

3.6   *Enter Lennox and another Lord.*

LENNOX
    My former speeches have but hit your thoughts,   1
    Which can interpret farther. Only I say   2
    Things have been strangely borne. The gracious Duncan 3
    Was pitied of Macbeth; marry, he was dead.   4
    And the right valiant Banquo walked too late,
    Whom you may say, if 't please you, Fleance killed,
    For Fleance fled. Men must not walk too late.
    Who cannot want the thought how monstrous   8
    It was for Malcolm and for Donalbain
    To kill their gracious father? Damnèd fact!   10
    How it did grieve Macbeth! Did he not straight   11
    In pious rage the two delinquents tear   12
    That were the slaves of drink and thralls of sleep?   13
    Was not that nobly done? Ay, and wisely too;
    For 'twould have angered any heart alive
    To hear the men deny 't. So that I say
    He has borne all things well; and I do think   17
    That had he Duncan's sons under his key—
    As, an 't please heaven, he shall not—they should find 19
    What 'twere to kill a father. So should Fleance.
    But peace! For from broad words, and 'cause he failed 21
    His presence at the tyrant's feast, I hear   22
    Macduff lives in disgrace. Sir, can you tell
    Where he bestows himself?   24
LORD   The son of Duncan,

3.6. Location: Somewhere in Scotland.
1 My former speeches what I've just said. **hit** coincided with
2 interpret farther draw further conclusions (i.e., it is unwise for me to
say more, but you can surmise the rest) **3 borne** carried on **4 of** by.
marry . . . dead i.e., to be sure, this pity occurred after Duncan died, not
before **8 cannot . . . thought** can help thinking **10 fact** deed, crime
11 straight straightway, at once **12 pious** holy, loyal, sonlike
13 thralls slaves **17 borne all things well** managed everything clev-
erly **19 an 't** if it. **should** would be sure to **21 from broad words** on
account of plain speech **22 His presence** i.e., to be present **24 bestows
himself** is quartered, has taken refuge

From whom this tyrant holds the due of birth,   25
Lives in the English court, and is received
Of the most pious Edward with such grace   27
That the malevolence of fortune nothing
Takes from his high respect. Thither Macduff   29
Is gone to pray the holy king, upon his aid,   30
To wake Northumberland and warlike Siward,
That by the help of these—with Him above
To ratify the work—we may again
Give to our tables meat, sleep to our nights,   34
Free from our feasts and banquets bloody knives,   35
Do faithful homage, and receive free honors—   36
All which we pine for now. And this report
Hath so exasperate the King that he   38
Prepares for some attempt of war.

LENNOX   Sent he to Macduff?

LORD

He did; and with an absolute "Sir, not I,"   41
The cloudy messenger turns me his back   42
And hums, as who should say, "You'll rue the time
That clogs me with this answer."

LENNOX   And that well might   44
Advise him to a caution, t' hold what distance   45
His wisdom can provide. Some holy angel   46
Fly to the court of England and unfold
His message ere he come, that a swift blessing
May soon return to this our suffering country   49
Under a hand accursed!   50

LORD   I'll send my prayers with him.   *Exeunt.*

❖

25 holds . . . birth withholds the birthright (i.e., the Scottish crown)   **27 Of**
by.   **Edward** Edward the Confessor   **29 his high respect** high respect paid
to him. (Being out of fortune has not lessened the dignity with which
Malcolm is received in England.)   **30 upon his aid** i.e., in aid of Malcolm
34 meat food   **35 Free . . . banquets** free our feasts and banquets from
36 free freely bestowed; or, pertaining to freemen   **38 exasperate the
King** i.e., exasperated Macbeth   **41 with . . . I** i.e., when Macduff answered the messenger curtly with a refusal   **42 cloudy** louring, scowling.
turns me i.e., turns. (*Me* is used colloquially for emphasis.)   **44 clogs**
encumbers, loads   **45–46 Advise . . . provide** warn him (Macduff) to keep
what safe distance he can (from Macbeth)   **49–50 suffering country
Under** country suffering under

4.1   *Thunder. Enter the three Witches.*

FIRST WITCH
Thrice the brinded cat hath mewed.   1

SECOND WITCH
Thrice, and once the hedgepig whined.   2

THIRD WITCH
Harpier cries. 'Tis time, 'tis time!   3

FIRST WITCH
Round about the cauldron go;
In the poisoned entrails throw.
Toad, that under cold stone
Days and nights has thirty-one   7
Sweltered venom, sleeping got,   8
Boil thou first i' the charmèd pot.

ALL [*As they dance round the cauldron*]
Double, double, toil and trouble;
Fire burn, and cauldron bubble.

SECOND WITCH
Fillet of a fenny snake   12
In the cauldron boil and bake;
Eye of newt and toe of frog,
Wool of bat and tongue of dog,
Adder's fork and blindworm's sting,   16
Lizard's leg and owlet's wing,
For a charm of powerful trouble,
Like a hell-broth boil and bubble.

ALL
Double, double, toil and trouble;
Fire burn, and cauldron bubble.

THIRD WITCH
Scale of dragon, tooth of wolf,
Witches' mummy, maw and gulf   23

4.1. Location: A cavern (see 3.5.15). In the middle, a boiling cauldron
(provided presumably by means of the trapdoor; see 4.1.106. The trapdoor must also be used in this scene for the apparitions.)
1 brinded marked by streaks (as by fire), brindled   **2 hedgepig** hedgehog
3 Harpier (The name of a familiar spirit; probably derived from *harpy*.)
cries i.e., gives the signal to begin   **7–8 Days . . . got** for thirty-one days
and nights has exuded venom formed during sleep   **12 Fillet** slice.   **fenny**
inhabiting fens or swamps   **16 fork** forked tongue.   **blindworm** slow-
worm, a harmless burrowing lizard   **23 mummy** mummified flesh
made into a magical potion.   **maw and gulf** gullet and stomach

Of the ravined salt-sea shark,   24
Root of hemlock digged i' the dark,
Liver of blaspheming Jew,
Gall of goat, and slips of yew   27
Slivered in the moon's eclipse,   28
Nose of Turk and Tartar's lips,
Finger of birth-strangled babe
Ditch-delivered by a drab,   31
Make the gruel thick and slab.   32
Add thereto a tiger's chaudron   33
For th' ingredients of our cauldron.

ALL
Double, double, toil and trouble;
Fire burn, and cauldron bubble.

SECOND WITCH
Cool it with a baboon's blood,
Then the charm is firm and good.   38

Enter Hecate to the other three Witches.

HECATE
O, well done! I commend your pains,   39
And everyone shall share i' the gains.
And now about the cauldron sing
Like elves and fairies in a ring,
Enchanting all that you put in.   43
            Music and a song: "Black spirits," *etc.*
                              [*Exit Hecate.*]

SECOND WITCH
By the pricking of my thumbs,
Something wicked this way comes.
      Open, locks,
      Whoever knocks!

Enter Macbeth.

24 ravined ravenous, glutted with prey (?) **27 slips** cuttings for grafting
or planting **28 Slivered** broken off (as a branch) **31 Ditch . . . drab**
born in a ditch of a harlot **32 slab** viscous, thick **33 chaudron** entrails **38 s.d. other** (Said because Hecate is a witch too, not because
more witches enter.) **39–43 O . . . in** (These lines are universally regarded as non-Shakespearean.) **43 s.d. Black spirits etc.** (This song is
found in Middleton's *The Witch.*)

MACBETH
   How now, you secret, black, and midnight hags?   48
   What is 't you do?
ALL   A deed without a name.
MACBETH
   I conjure you, by that which you profess,
   Howe'er you come to know it, answer me.
   Though you untie the winds and let them fight
   Against the churches, though the yeasty waves   53
   Confound and swallow navigation up,   54
   Though bladed corn be lodged and trees blown down, 55
   Though castles topple on their warders' heads,
   Though palaces and pyramids do slope   57
   Their heads to their foundations, though the treasure
   Of nature's germens tumble all together,   59
   Even till destruction sicken, answer me   60
   To what I ask you.
FIRST WITCH   Speak.
SECOND WITCH   Demand.
THIRD WITCH   We'll answer.
FIRST WITCH
   Say if thou'dst rather hear it from our mouths
   Or from our masters.
MACBETH   Call 'em. Let me see 'em.
FIRST WITCH
   Pour in sow's blood, that hath eaten
   Her nine farrow; grease that's sweaten   65
   From the murderer's gibbet throw
   Into the flame.
ALL   Come high or low,
   Thyself and office deftly show!   68

Thunder. First Apparition, an armed Head.

MACBETH
   Tell me, thou unknown power—

---

48 black i.e., dealing in black magic   **53 yeasty** foamy   **54 Confound**
destroy   **55 bladed** in the ear.   **corn** (General name for wheat and other
grains.)   **lodged** thrown down, laid   **57 slope** bend   **59 nature's germens** seed or elements from which all nature operates   **60 sicken** be
surfeited   **65 nine farrow** litter of nine.   **sweaten** sweated   **68 office**
function   **s.d. armed Head** (Perhaps symbolizes the head of Macbeth
cut off by Macduff and presented by him to Malcolm; or the rebellion
of Macduff.)

FIRST WITCH   He knows thy thought.
  Hear his speech, but say thou naught.
FIRST APPARITION
  Macbeth! Macbeth! Macbeth! Beware Macduff,
  Beware the Thane of Fife. Dismiss me. Enough.   72
                                        He descends.

MACBETH
  Whate'er thou art, for thy good caution, thanks;
  Thou hast harped my fear aright. But one word more—   74
FIRST WITCH
  He will not be commanded. Here's another,
  More potent than the first.   76

          Thunder. Second Apparition, a bloody Child.

SECOND APPARITION   Macbeth! Macbeth! Macbeth!
MACBETH   Had I three ears, I'd hear thee.
SECOND APPARITION
  Be bloody, bold, and resolute; laugh to scorn
  The power of man, for none of woman born
  Shall harm Macbeth.   *Descends.*
MACBETH
  Then live, Macduff; what need I fear of thee?
  But yet I'll make assurance double sure,
  And take a bond of fate. Thou shalt not live,   84
  That I may tell pale-hearted fear it lies,
  And sleep in spite of thunder.   86

          *Thunder. Third Apparition, a Child crowned,
          with a tree in his hand.*

                              What is this
  That rises like the issue of a king   87
  And wears upon his baby brow the round   88
  And top of sovereignty?
ALL   Listen, but speak not to 't.   89

---

72 s.d. He descends (i.e., by means of the trap door)   **74 harped** hit,
touched (as in touching a harp to make it sound)   **76 s.d. bloody Child**
(Symbolizes Macduff untimely ripped from his mother's womb; see
5.8.15–16.)   **84 take a bond of** get a guarantee from (i.e., by killing
Macduff, to make doubly sure he can do no harm)   **86 s.d. Child . . .
hand** (Symbolizes Malcolm, the royal child; the tree anticipates the
cutting of boughs in Birnam Wood, 5.4.)   **87 like** in the likeness of
88–89 round And top crown

THIRD APPARITION
  Be lion-mettled, proud, and take no care
  Who chafes, who frets, or where conspirers are.
  Macbeth shall never vanquished be until
  Great Birnam Wood to high Dunsinane Hill
  Shall come against him.   *Descends.*
MACBETH   That will never be.
  Who can impress the forest, bid the tree   95
  Unfix his earthbound root? Sweet bodements, good!   96
  Rebellious dead, rise never till the wood   97
  Of Birnam rise, and our high-placed Macbeth
  Shall live the lease of nature, pay his breath   99
  To time and mortal custom. Yet my heart   100
  Throbs to know one thing. Tell me, if your art
  Can tell so much: shall Banquo's issue ever
  Reign in this kingdom?
ALL   Seek to know no more.
MACBETH
  I will be satisfied. Deny me this,
  And an eternal curse fall on you! Let me know.
                [The cauldron descends.] Hautboys.
  Why sinks that cauldron? And what noise is this?   106
FIRST WITCH   Show!
SECOND WITCH   Show!
THIRD WITCH   Show!
ALL
  Show his eyes, and grieve his heart;
  Come like shadows, so depart!   111

       *A show of eight Kings and Banquo last; [the
       eighth King] with a glass in his hand.*

MACBETH
  Thou art too like the spirit of Banquo. Down!
  Thy crown does sear mine eyeballs. And thy hair,
  Thou other gold-bound brow, is like the first.   114
  A third is like the former. Filthy hags,
  Why do you show me this? A fourth? Start, eyes!   116

95 impress press into service, like soldiers   **96 bodements** prophecies
97 Rebellious dead i.e., Banquo and his lineage (?)   **99 lease of nature**
natural period, full life-span   **100 mortal custom** death, the common lot
of humanity   **106 noise** music   **111 s.d. glass** (magic) mirror (also in
l. 119)   **114 other** i.e., second   **116 Start** bulge from their sockets

What, will the line stretch out to th' crack of doom?
Another yet? A seventh? I'll see no more.
And yet the eighth appears, who bears a glass
Which shows me many more; and some I see
That twofold balls and treble scepters carry.   121
Horrible sight! Now I see 'tis true,
For the blood-boltered Banquo smiles upon me   123
And points at them for his. [*The apparitions vanish.*]
    What, is this so?   124

FIRST WITCH
    Ay, sir, all this is so. But why   125
    Stands Macbeth thus amazedly?   126
    Come, sisters, cheer we up his sprites   127
    And show the best of our delights.
    I'll charm the air to give a sound,
    While you perform your antic round,   130
    That this great king may kindly say
    Our duties did his welcome pay.   132
            Music. The Witches dance, and vanish.

MACBETH
    Where are they? Gone? Let this pernicious hour
    Stand aye accursèd in the calendar!
    Come in, without there!

        Enter Lennox.

LENNOX   What's Your Grace's will?
MACBETH
    Saw you the Weird Sisters?
LENNOX   No, my lord.
MACBETH
    Came they not by you?
LENNOX   No, indeed, my lord.

121 **twofold balls** (A probable reference to the double coronation of
James at Scone and Westminster, as King of England and Scotland.)
treble scepters (Probably refers to James's assumed title as King of
Great Britain, France, and Ireland.)   123 **blood-boltered** having his hair
matted with blood   124 **for his** as his descendants   125–132 **Ay . . . pay**
(These lines are held to be spurious.)   126 **amazedly** stunned
127 **sprites** spirits   130 **antic round** grotesque dance in a circle
132 **pay** repay

MACBETH
  Infected be the air whereon they ride,
  And damned all those that trust them! I did hear
  The galloping of horse. Who was 't came by?   140

LENNOX
  'Tis two or three, my lord, that bring you word
  Macduff is fled to England.

MACBETH   Fled to England!

LENNOX   Ay, my good lord.

MACBETH [*Aside*]
  Time, thou anticipat'st my dread exploits.   144
  The flighty purpose never is o'ertook   145
  Unless the deed go with it. From this moment   146
  The very firstlings of my heart shall be   147
  The firstlings of my hand. And even now,   148
  To crown my thoughts with acts, be it thought and done:
  The castle of Macduff I will surprise,   150
  Seize upon Fife, give to th' edge o' the sword
  His wife, his babes, and all unfortunate souls
  That trace him in his line. No boasting like a fool;   153
  This deed I'll do before this purpose cool.
  But no more sights!—Where are these gentlemen?
  Come, bring me where they are.   *Exeunt.*

❖

4.2   *Enter Macduff's Wife, her Son, and Ross.*

LADY MACDUFF
  What had he done to make him fly the land?

ROSS
  You must have patience, madam.

LADY MACDUFF   He had none.

---

140 horse horses   **144 thou anticipat'st** you forestall. (By allowing time to pass without my acting, I have lost an opportunity.)   **145 flighty** fleeting   **146 Unless . . . it** unless the execution of the deed accompanies the conception of it immediately   **147–148 The very . . . hand** i.e., my impulses will be acted on immediately   **150 surprise** seize without warning   **153 trace him** follow his tracks.   **line** family succession

4.2. Location: Fife. Macduff's castle.

His flight was madness. When our actions do not,   3
Our fears do make us traitors.

ROSS   You know not   4
Whether it was his wisdom or his fear.

LADY MACDUFF
Wisdom? To leave his wife, to leave his babes,
His mansion, and his titles in a place   7
From whence himself does fly? He loves us not,
He wants the natural touch; for the poor wren,   9
The most diminutive of birds, will fight,
Her young ones in her nest, against the owl.   11
All is the fear and nothing is the love,
As little is the wisdom, where the flight
So runs against all reason.

ROSS   My dearest coz,   14
I pray you, school yourself. But, for your husband,   15
He is noble, wise, judicious, and best knows
The fits o' the season. I dare not speak much further,   17
But cruel are the times when we are traitors   18
And do not know ourselves, when we hold rumor   19
From what we fear, yet know not what we fear,   20
But float upon a wild and violent sea
Each way and none. I take my leave of you;   22
Shall not be long but I'll be here again.   23
Things at the worst will cease, or else climb upward
To what they were before.—My pretty cousin,
Blessing upon you!

LADY MACDUFF
Fathered he is, and yet he's fatherless.

ROSS
I am so much a fool, should I stay longer

3–4 When . . . traitors i.e., even when we have committed no treasonous
act, our fears of being suspected traitors make us act as if we were
7 titles i.e., possessions to which he has title   **9 wants** lacks.   **the**
natural touch i.e., the feelings natural to a husband and father   **11 Her**
. . . nest when her young ones are in the nest   **14 coz** kinswoman
15 school control.   **for** as for   **17 fits 'o the season** violent disorders of
the time   **18–19 are traitors . . . ourselves** i.e., are accused of treason
without recognizing ourselves as such   **19–20 hold . . . fear** i.e., believe
every fearful rumor on the basis of what we fear might be   **22 Each . . .**
none i.e., being tossed this way and that without any real progress
23 Shall it shall.   **but** before

It would be my disgrace and your discomfort.   29
I take my leave at once.   *Exit Ross.*

LADY MACDUFF   Sirrah, your father's dead;   31
And what will you do now? How will you live?

SON
As birds do, Mother.

LADY MACDUFF   What, with worms and flies?

SON
With what I get, I mean; and so do they.

LADY MACDUFF   Poor bird! Thou'dst never fear
The net nor lime, the pitfall nor the gin.   36

SON
Why should I, Mother? Poor birds they are not set for. 37
My father is not dead, for all your saying.

LADY MACDUFF
Yes, he is dead. How wilt thou do for a father?

SON   Nay, how will you do for a husband?

LADY MACDUFF   Why, I can buy me twenty at any
market.

SON   Then you'll buy 'em to sell again.

LADY MACDUFF   Thou speak'st with all thy wit,
And yet, i' faith, with wit enough for thee.

SON   Was my father a traitor, Mother?

LADY MACDUFF   Ay, that he was.

SON   What is a traitor?

LADY MACDUFF   Why, one that swears and lies.   49

SON   And be all traitors that do so?

LADY MACDUFF
Every one that does so is a traitor,
And must be hanged.

SON
And must they all be hanged that swear and lie?

LADY MACDUFF   Every one.

SON   Who must hang them?

LADY MACDUFF   Why, the honest men.

SON   Then the liars and swearers are fools, for there are

---

29 It . . . discomfort i.e., I should disgrace my manhood by weeping, and
cause you distress   **31 Sirrah** (Here, an affectionate form of address to
a child.)   **36 lime** birdlime (a sticky substance put on branches to snare
birds).   **gin** snare   **37 Poor . . . for** i.e., traps are not set for *poor* birds,
as you call me   **49 swears and lies** i.e., swears an oath and breaks it
(though the boy may understand *swears* to mean "uses profanity")

liars and swearers enough to beat the honest men and
hang up them.

LADY MACDUFF   Now, God help thee, poor monkey! But
how wilt thou do for a father?

SON   If he were dead, you'd weep for him; if you would
not, it were a good sign that I should quickly have a
new father.

LADY MACDUFF   Poor prattler, how thou talk'st!

Enter a Messenger.

MESSENGER
  Bless you, fair dame! I am not to you known,
  Though in your state of honor I am perfect.   67
  I doubt some danger does approach you nearly.   68
  If you will take a homely man's advice,   69
  Be not found here. Hence with your little ones!
  To fright you thus, methinks, I am too savage;
  To do worse to you were fell cruelty,   72
  Which is too nigh your person. Heaven preserve you!   73
  I dare abide no longer.   *Exit Messenger.*

LADY MACDUFF   Whither should I fly?
  I have done no harm. But I remember now
  I am in this earthly world, where to do harm
  Is often laudable, to do good sometimes
  Accounted dangerous folly. Why then, alas,
  Do I put up that womanly defense
  To say I have done no harm?

Enter Murderers.

                              What are these faces?

FIRST MURDERER   Where is your husband?

LADY MACDUFF
  I hope in no place so unsanctified
  Where such as thou mayst find him.

FIRST MURDERER   He's a traitor.

SON
  Thou liest, thou shag-haired villain!

---

67 in . . . honor with your honorable state.   **perfect** perfectly ac-
quainted   **68 doubt** fear   **69 homely** plain   **72 To do worse** i.e., actually
to harm you.   **fell** savage   **73 Which . . . person** i.e., which savage
cruelty is all too near at hand

FIRST MURDERER   What, you egg?
                                             [*He stabs him.*]
  Young fry of treachery!
SON   He has killed me, Mother.   85
  Run away, I pray you!   [*He dies.*]
            Exit [*Lady Macduff*] *crying "Murder!"* [*followed
                by the Murderers with the Son's body*].

                              ❖

4.3   *Enter Malcolm and Macduff.*

MALCOLM
  Let us seek out some desolate shade, and there
  Weep our sad bosoms empty.
MACDUFF   Let us rather
  Hold fast the mortal sword, and like good men   3
  Bestride our downfall'n birthdom. Each new morn   4
  New widows howl, new orphans cry, new sorrows
  Strike heaven on the face, that it resounds   6
  As if it felt with Scotland and yelled out   7
  Like syllable of dolor.
MALCOLM   What I believe, I'll wail;   8
  What know, believe; and what I can redress,   9
  As I shall find the time to friend, I will.   10
  What you have spoke it may be so, perchance.
  This tyrant, whose sole name blisters our tongues,   12
  Was once thought honest. You have loved him well;
  He hath not touched you yet. I am young; but something 14
  You may deserve of him through me, and wisdom   15

85 **fry** spawn, progeny

4.3. Location: England. Before King Edward the Confessor's palace.
3 mortal deadly   **4 Bestride** stand over in defense.   **birthdom** native
land   **6 Strike . . . face** offer an insulting slap in the face to heaven
itself.   **that it resounds** so that it echoes   **7–8 As . . . dolor** as if heaven,
feeling itself the blow delivered to Scotland, cried out with a similar cry
of pain   **8 Like** similar   **8–9 What . . . believe** i.e., what I believe to be
amiss in Scotland I will grieve for, and anything I am certain to be true
I will believe. (But one must be cautious in these duplicitous times.)
10 to friend opportune   **12 sole** mere   **14 He . . . yet** i.e., the fact that
Macbeth hasn't hurt you yet makes me suspicious of your loyalties.
young i.e., inexperienced   **14–15 something . . . me** i.e., you may win
favor with Macbeth by delivering me to him   **15 wisdom** i.e., it would
be worldly-wise

To offer up a weak, poor, innocent lamb
T' appease an angry god.
MACDUFF   I am not treacherous.
MALCOLM   But Macbeth is.
A good and virtuous nature may recoil   20
In an imperial charge. But I shall crave your pardon.   21
That which you are my thoughts cannot transpose;   22
Angels are bright still, though the brightest fell.   23
Though all things foul would wear the brows of grace,   24
Yet grace must still look so.
MACDUFF   I have lost my hopes.   25
MALCOLM
Perchance even there where I did find my doubts.   26
Why in that rawness left you wife and child,   27
Those precious motives, those strong knots of love,   28
Without leave-taking? I pray you,
Let not my jealousies be your dishonors,   30
But mine own safeties. You may be rightly just,   31
Whatever I shall think.
MACDUFF   Bleed, bleed, poor country!
Great tyranny, lay thou thy basis sure,   33
For goodness dare not check thee; wear thou thy wrongs, 34
The title is affeered! Fare thee well, lord.   35
I would not be the villain that thou think'st
For the whole space that's in the tyrant's grasp,

20 recoil give way, fall back (as in the firing of a gun)   **21 In . . . charge**
under pressure from royal command. (*Charge* puns on the idea of a
quantity of powder and shot for a gun, as in *recoil*.)   **22 That . . . transpose** my suspicious thoughts cannot change you from what you are,
cannot make you evil   **23 the brightest** i.e., Lucifer   **24–25 Though . . .
so** i.e., even though evil puts on the appearance of good so often as to
cast that appearance into deep suspicion, yet goodness must go on
looking and acting like itself   **25 hopes** i.e., hopes of Malcolm's assistance in the cause against Macbeth   **26 Perchance even there** i.e.,
perhaps in that same mistrustful frame of mind.   **doubts** i.e., fears
such as that Macduff may covertly be on Macbeth's side   **27 rawness**
unprotected condition. (Malcolm suggests that Macduff's leaving his
family unprotected could be construed as more evidence of his not
having anything to fear from Macbeth.)   **28 motives** persons inspiring
you to cherish and protect them; incentives to offer strong protection
30–31 Let . . . safeties i.e., may it be true that my suspicions of your
lack of honor are founded only in my own wariness   **33 basis** founda-
tion   **34 wrongs** wrongfully gained powers   **35 affeered** confirmed,
certified

And the rich East to boot.
MALCOLM   Be not offended.   38
  I speak not as in absolute fear of you.   39
  I think our country sinks beneath the yoke;   40
  It weeps, it bleeds, and each new day a gash
  Is added to her wounds. I think withal   42
  There would be hands uplifted in my right;   43
  And here from gracious England have I offer   44
  Of goodly thousands. But, for all this,
  When I shall tread upon the tyrant's head,
  Or wear it on my sword, yet my poor country
  Shall have more vices than it had before,
  More suffer, and more sundry ways than ever,   49
  By him that shall succeed.
MACDUFF   What should he be?   50
MALCOLM
  It is myself I mean, in whom I know
  All the particulars of vice so grafted   52
  That, when they shall be opened, black Macbeth   53
  Will seem as pure as snow, and the poor state
  Esteem him as a lamb, being compared
  With my confineless harms.
MACDUFF   Not in the legions   56
  Of horrid hell can come a devil more damned
  In evils to top Macbeth.
MALCOLM   I grant him bloody,   58
  Luxurious, avaricious, false, deceitful,   59
  Sudden, malicious, smacking of every sin   60
  That has a name. But there's no bottom, none,
  In my voluptuousness. Your wives, your daughters,
  Your matrons, and your maids could not fill up
  The cistern of my lust, and my desire
  All continent impediments would o'erbear   65
  That did oppose my will. Better Macbeth   66

38 to boot in addition   **39 absolute fear** complete mistrust   **40 think**
am mindful that   **42 withal** in addition   **43 right** cause   **44 England**
i.e., the King of England   **49 more sundry** in more various   **50 What**
who   **52 particulars** varieties.   **grafted** (1) engrafted, indissolubly mixed
(2) grafted like a plant that will then *open* or unfold   **53 opened** un-
folded (like a bud)   **56 my confineless harms** the boundless injuries I
shall inflict   **58 top** surpass   **59 Luxurious** lecherous   **60 Sudden**
violent, passionate   **65 continent** (1) chaste (2) restraining, containing
66 will lust (also in l. 89)

Than such an one to reign.
MACDUFF   Boundless intemperance
In nature is a tyranny; it hath been   68
Th' untimely emptying of the happy throne
And fall of many kings. But fear not yet   70
To take upon you what is yours. You may
Convey your pleasures in a spacious plenty,   72
And yet seem cold; the time you may so hoodwink.   73
We have willing dames enough. There cannot be
That vulture in you to devour so many
As will to greatness dedicate themselves,
Finding it so inclined.
MALCOLM   With this there grows
In my most ill-composed affection such   78
A stanchless avarice that, were I king,   79
I should cut off the nobles for their lands,
Desire his jewels and this other's house,   81
And my more-having would be as a sauce
To make me hunger more, that I should forge   83
Quarrels unjust against the good and loyal,
Destroying them for wealth.
MACDUFF   This avarice
Sticks deeper, grows with more pernicious root
Than summer-seeming lust, and it hath been   87
The sword of our slain kings. Yet do not fear;   88
Scotland hath foisons to fill up your will   89
Of your mere own. All these are portable,   90
With other graces weighed.   91
MALCOLM
But I have none. The king-becoming graces,
As justice, verity, temperance, stableness,
Bounty, perseverance, mercy, lowliness,   94
Devotion, patience, courage, fortitude,
I have no relish of them, but abound   96

68 nature human nature   **70 yet** nevertheless   **72 Convey** manage with
secrecy   **73 cold** chaste.   **the time . . . hoodwink** you may so deceive
the age.   **hoodwink** blindfold   **78 ill-composed affection** evil disposition   **79 stanchless** insatiable   **81 his** one man's.   **this other's** another's   **83 that** so that   **87 summer-seeming** appropriate to youth (and
lessening in later years)   **88 sword** i.e., cause of overthrow   **89 foisons**
resources, plenty   **90 Of . . . own** i.e., in your own royal estates alone.
portable bearable   **91 weighed** counterbalanced   **94 lowliness** humil-
ity   **96 relish** flavor or trace

In the division of each several crime,   97
Acting it many ways. Nay, had I power, I should
Pour the sweet milk of concord into hell,
Uproar the universal peace, confound   100
All unity on earth.
MACDUFF   O Scotland, Scotland!
MALCOLM
If such a one be fit to govern, speak.
I am as I have spoken.
MACDUFF   Fit to govern?
No, not to live. O nation miserable,
With an untitled tyrant bloody-sceptered,   105
When shalt thou see thy wholesome days again,
Since that the truest issue of thy throne
By his own interdiction stands accursed   108
And does blaspheme his breed? Thy royal father   109
Was a most sainted king; the queen that bore thee,
Oft'ner upon her knees than on her feet,
Died every day she lived. Fare thee well.   112
These evils thou repeat'st upon thyself
Hath banished me from Scotland. O my breast,   114
Thy hope ends here!
MALCOLM   Macduff, this noble passion,
Child of integrity, hath from my soul   116
Wiped the black scruples, reconciled my thoughts
To thy good truth and honor. Devilish Macbeth
By many of these trains hath sought to win me   119
Into his power, and modest wisdom plucks me   120
From overcredulous haste. But God above
Deal between thee and me! For even now
I put myself to thy direction and
Unspeak mine own detraction, here abjure   124
The taints and blames I laid upon myself
For strangers to my nature. I am yet   126

---

97 division subdivisions, various possible forms.   **several** separate
100 Uproar throw into an uproar   **105 untitled** lacking rightful title,
usurping   **108 interdiction** debarring of self   **109 blaspheme** slander,
defame.   **breed** breeding (i.e., he is a disgrace to his royal lineage)
112 Died . . . lived i.e., lived a life of daily mortification   **114 breast**
heart   **116 Child of integrity** a product of your integrity of spirit
119 trains plots, artifices   **120 modest . . . me** wise prudence holds me
back   **124 mine own detraction** my detraction of myself   **126 For** as

Unknown to woman, never was forsworn,   127
Scarcely have coveted what was mine own,
At no time broke my faith, would not betray
The devil to his fellow, and delight
No less in truth than life. My first false speaking
Was this upon myself. What I am truly   132
Is thine and my poor country's to command—
Whither indeed, before thy here-approach,
Old Siward with ten thousand warlike men,
Already at a point, was setting forth.   136
Now we'll together; and the chance of goodness   137
Be like our warranted quarrel! Why are you silent?   138

MACDUFF
Such welcome and unwelcome things at once
'Tis hard to reconcile.

    Enter a Doctor.

MALCOLM
Well, more anon.—Comes the King forth, I pray you?

DOCTOR
Ay, sir. There are a crew of wretched souls
That stay his cure. Their malady convinces   143
The great assay of art; but at his touch—   144
Such sanctity hath heaven given his hand—
They presently amend.

MALCOLM   I thank you, Doctor.   146

                        Exit [Doctor].

MACDUFF
What's the disease he means?

MALCOLM   'Tis called the evil.   147
A most miraculous work in this good king,
Which often, since my here-remain in England,   149
I have seen him do. How he solicits heaven   150
Himself best knows; but strangely-visited people,   151

---

127 Unknown to woman a virgin   **132 upon** against   **136 at a point**
ready, prepared   **137 the chance of goodness** may the chance of success   **138 Be . . . quarrel** be proportionate to the justice of our cause
143 stay wait for.   **convinces** conquers   **144 assay of art** efforts of
medical skill   **146 presently** immediately   **147 evil** i.e., scrofula, supposedly cured by the royal touch; James I claimed this power   **149 here-
remain** stay   **150 solicits** prevails by prayer with   **151 strangely-visited**
afflicted by strange diseases

All swoll'n and ulcerous, pitiful to the eye,
The mere despair of surgery, he cures,   153
Hanging a golden stamp about their necks   154
Put on with holy prayers; and 'tis spoken,
To the succeeding royalty he leaves
The healing benediction. With this strange virtue   157
He hath a heavenly gift of prophecy,
And sundry blessings hang about his throne
That speak him full of grace.

    Enter Ross.

MACDUFF   See who comes here.
MALCOLM
My countryman, but yet I know him not.   161
MACDUFF
My ever-gentle cousin, welcome hither.   162
MALCOLM
I know him now. Good God betimes remove   163
The means that makes us strangers!
ROSS   Sir, amen.
MACDUFF
Stands Scotland where it did?
ROSS   Alas, poor country,
Almost afraid to know itself. It cannot
Be called our mother, but our grave; where nothing   167
But who knows nothing is once seen to smile;   168
Where sighs and groans and shrieks that rend the air
Are made, not marked; where violent sorrow seems   170
A modern ecstasy. The dead man's knell   171
Is there scarce asked for who, and good men's lives
Expire before the flowers in their caps,
Dying or ere they sicken.
MACDUFF   O, relation   174
Too nice, and yet too true!
MALCOLM   What's the newest grief?   175

---

153 mere utter   **154 stamp** minted coin   **157 virtue** healing power
161 My countryman (So identified by his dress.)   **know** recognize
162 gentle noble   **163 betimes** speedily   **167 nothing** nobody   **168 But
who** except a person who.   **once** ever   **170 marked** noticed (because
they are so common)   **171 modern ecstasy** commonplace emotion
174 or ere they sicken before they have had time to fall ill.   **relation**
report   **175 nice** minutely accurate, elaborately phrased

ROSS
  That of an hour's age doth hiss the speaker;   176
  Each minute teems a new one.
MACDUFF   How does my wife?   177
ROSS
  Why, well.
MACDUFF   And all my children?
ROSS   Well too.   178
MACDUFF
  The tyrant has not battered at their peace?
ROSS
  No, they were well at peace when I did leave 'em.
MACDUFF
  Be not a niggard of your speech. How goes 't?
ROSS
  When I came hither to transport the tidings
  Which I have heavily borne, there ran a rumor   183
  Of many worthy fellows that were out,   184
  Which was to my belief witnessed the rather   185
  For that I saw the tyrant's power afoot.   186
  Now is the time of help; your eye in Scotland
  Would create soldiers, make our women fight,
  To doff their dire distresses.
MALCOLM   Be 't their comfort   189
  We are coming thither. Gracious England hath   190
  Lent us good Siward and ten thousand men;
  An older and a better soldier none
  That Christendom gives out.
ROSS   Would I could answer   193
  This comfort with the like! But I have words
  That would be howled out in the desert air,
  Where hearing should not latch them.
MACDUFF   What concern they?   196
  The general cause? Or is it a fee-grief   197

---

176 hiss cause to be hissed (for repeating stale news)   **177 teems** teems
with, yields   **178 Well** (Ross quibbles, in his reluctance to tell the bad
news, on the saying that "the dead are well," i.e., at rest.)   **183 heavily**
sadly   **184 out** in arms, in the field   **185 witnessed the rather** made
the more believable   **186 power** army   **189 doff** put off, get rid of
190 Gracious England i.e., Edward the Confessor   **193 gives out** tells of,
proclaims   **196 latch** catch (the sound of)   **197 fee-grief** a grief with an
individual owner, having absolute ownership

Due to some single breast?

ROSS   No mind that's honest   198
But in it shares some woe, though the main part
Pertains to you alone.

MACDUFF   If it be mine,
Keep it not from me; quickly let me have it.

ROSS
Let not your ears despise my tongue forever,
Which shall possess them with the heaviest sound   203
That ever yet they heard.

MACDUFF   Hum! I guess at it.

ROSS
Your castle is surprised, your wife and babes
Savagely slaughtered. To relate the manner
Were, on the quarry of these murdered deer,   207
To add the death of you.

MALCOLM   Merciful heaven!
What, man, ne'er pull your hat upon your brows;   209
Give sorrow words. The grief that does not speak
Whispers the o'erfraught heart and bids it break.   211

MACDUFF
My children too?

ROSS   Wife, children, servants, all
That could be found.

MACDUFF   And I must be from thence! 213
My wife killed too?

ROSS   I have said.

MALCOLM   Be comforted.
Let's make us medicines of our great revenge
To cure this deadly grief.

MACDUFF
He has no children. All my pretty ones?   217
Did you say all? O hell-kite! All?
What, all my pretty chickens and their dam
At one fell swoop?   220

---

198 Due to i.e., owned by   **203 possess them with** put them in posses-
sion of   **207 quarry** heap of slaughtered deer at a hunt (with a pun on
dear, deer)   **209 pull your hat** (A conventional gesture of grief.)
211 Whispers whispers to.   **o'erfraught** overburdened   **213 must** had
to   **217 He has no children** i.e., no father would do such a thing (?), or,
he (Malcolm) speaks comfort without knowing what such a loss feels
like (?)   **220 fell swoop** cruel swoop of the *hell-kite*, bird of prey from
hell (with a suggestion too of swoopstake, sweepstake)

MALCOLM   Dispute it like a man.   221
MACDUFF   I shall do so;
  But I must also feel it as a man.
  I cannot but remember such things were,
  That were most precious to me. Did heaven look on
  And would not take their part? Sinful Macduff,
  They were all struck for thee! Naught that I am,.   227
  Not for their own demerits, but for mine,
  Fell slaughter on their souls. Heaven rest them now!
MALCOLM
  Be this the whetstone of your sword. Let grief
  Convert to anger; blunt not the heart, enrage it.   231
MACDUFF
  O, I could play the woman with mine eyes
  And braggart with my tongue! But, gentle heavens,
  Cut short all intermission. Front to front   234
  Bring thou this fiend of Scotland and myself;
  Within my sword's length set him. If he scape,
  Heaven forgive him too!
MALCOLM   This tune goes manly.   237
  Come, go we to the King. Our power is ready;   238
  Our lack is nothing but our leave. Macbeth   239
  Is ripe for shaking, and the powers above
  Put on their instruments. Receive what cheer you may. 241
  The night is long that never finds the day.   *Exeut.*

✤

---

221 Dispute it i.e., fight on the issue; or, be a man, don't give in to
grief   **227 for thee** i.e., as divine punishment for your sins.   **Naught**
wicked   **231 Convert** change   **234 intermission** delay, interval.   **Front
to front** face to face   **237 too** i.e., as I would have had to forgive him
before allowing him to escape. (Macduff's point is that Macbeth will
never escape, since these conditions will never be met.)   **238 power**
army   **239 Our . . . leave** we need only to take our leave (of the English
King)   **241 Put . . . instruments** set us on as their agents; or, arm
themselves

5.1   *Enter a Doctor of Physic and a*
          Waïting-Gentlewoman.

DOCTOR   I have two nights watched with you, but can
perceive no truth in your report. When was it she last
walked?

GENTLEWOMAN   Since His Majesty went into the field, I
have seen her rise from her bed, throw her nightgown
upon her, unlock her closet, take forth paper, fold it, 5
write upon 't, read it, afterwards seal it, and again return to bed; yet all this while in a most fast sleep.

DOCTOR   A great perturbation in nature, to receive at
once the benefit of sleep and do the effects of watch- 9
ing! In this slumbery agitation, besides her walking 10
and other actual performances, what, at any time,
have you heard her say?

GENTLEWOMAN   That, sir, which I will not report after her.

DOCTOR   You may to me, and 'tis most meet you should.

GENTLEWOMAN   Neither to you nor anyone, having no
witness to confirm my speech.

          Enter Lady [Macbeth], with a taper.

Lo you, here she comes! This is her very guise, and,
upon my life, fast asleep. Observe her. Stand close.   19
                              [*They stand aside.*]

DOCTOR   How came she by that light?

GENTLEWOMAN   Why, it stood by her. She has light by
her continually. 'Tis her command.

DOCTOR   You see her eyes are open.

GENTLEWOMAN   Ay, but their sense are shut.

DOCTOR   What is it she does now? Look how she rubs
her hands.

GENTLEWOMAN   It is an accustomed action with her to
seem thus washing her hands. I have known her continue in this a quarter of an hour.

LADY MACBETH   Yet here's a spot.

DOCTOR   Hark, she speaks. I will set down what comes

5.1. Location: Dunsinane. Macbeth's castle.
5 closet chest or desk   **9–10 effects of watching** deeds characteristic of
waking   **10 agitation** activity   **19 close** concealed

from her, to satisfy my remembrance the more 32
strongly.

LADY MACBETH Out, damned spot! Out, I say! One—
two—why then, 'tis time to do 't. Hell is murky.—
Fie, my lord, fie, a soldier, and afeard? What need we
fear who knows it, when none can call our power to
account? Yet who would have thought the old man to
have had so much blood in him?

DOCTOR Do you mark that?

LADY MACBETH The Thane of Fife had a wife. Where is
she now?—What, will these hands ne'er be clean?—
No more o' that, my lord, no more o' that; you mar all
with this starting.   44

DOCTOR Go to, go to. You have known what you should
not.

GENTLEWOMAN She has spoke what she should not, I
am sure of that. Heaven knows what she has known.

LADY MACBETH Here's the smell of the blood still. All
the perfumes of Arabia will not sweeten this little
hand. O, O, O!

DOCTOR What a sigh is there! The heart is sorely 52
charged.   53

GENTLEWOMAN I would not have such a heart in my
bosom for the dignity of the whole body.   55

DOCTOR Well, well, well.

GENTLEWOMAN Pray God it be, sir.

DOCTOR This disease is beyond my practice. Yet I have
known those which have walked in their sleep who
have died holily in their beds.

LADY MACBETH Wash your hands, put on your nightgown; look not so pale! I tell you yet again, Banquo's
buried. He cannot come out on 's grave.   63

DOCTOR Even so?

LADY MACBETH To bed, to bed! There's knocking at the
gate. Come, come, come, come, give me your hand.
What's done cannot be undone. To bed, to bed,
to bed!   *Exit Lady.*

DOCTOR Will she go now to bed?

---

32 satisfy confirm, support **44 this starting** these startled move-
ments **52–53 sorely charged** heavily burdened **55 dignity** worth,
value **63 on 's** of his

GENTLEWOMAN   Directly.

DOCTOR
  Foul whisperings are abroad. Unnatural deeds
  Do breed unnatural troubles. Infected minds
  To their deaf pillows will discharge their secrets.
  More needs she the divine than the physician.
  God, God forgive us all! Look after her;
  Remove from her the means of all annoyance,   76
  And still keep eyes upon her. So, good night.   77
  My mind she has mated, and amazed my sight.   78
  I think, but dare not speak.
GENTLEWOMAN   Good night, good Doctor.
                                 Exeunt.

❖

5.2   *Drum and colors. Enter Menteith, Caithness,*
      Angus, Lennox, [and] soldiers.

MENTEITH
  The English power is near, led on by Malcolm,
  His uncle Siward, and the good Macduff.
  Revenges burn in them, for their dear causes   3
  Would to the bleeding and the grim alarm   4
  Excite the mortified man.
ANGUS   Near Birnam Wood   5
  Shall we well meet them; that way are they coming.   6
CAITHNESS
  Who knows if Donalbain be with his brother?
LENNOX
  For certain, sir, he is not. I have a file   8
  Of all the gentry. There is Siward's son,
  And many unrough youths that even now   10
  Protest their first of manhood.
MENTEITH   What does the tyrant?   11

---

76 annoyance i.e., harming herself   **77 still** constantly   **78 mated**
bewildered, stupefied

5.2. Location: The country near Dunsinane.
3 dear heartfelt, grievous   **4 bleeding** bloody.   **alarm** call to battle
5 Excite . . . man awaken the dead   **6 well** no doubt   **8 file** list, roster
10 unrough beardless   **11 Protest** assert publicly

CAITHNESS
　Great Dunsinane he strongly fortifies.
　Some say he's mad, others that lesser hate him
　Do call it valiant fury; but for certain
　He cannot buckle his distempered cause   15
　Within the belt of rule.
ANGUS　　　　　　　　Now does he feel
　His secret murders sticking on his hands;
　Now minutely revolts upbraid his faith-breach.   18
　Those he commands move only in command,   19
　Nothing in love. Now does he feel his title
　Hang loose about him, like a giant's robe
　Upon a dwarfish thief.
MENTEITH　　　　　　　Who then shall blame
　His pestered senses to recoil and start,   23
　When all that is within him does condemn
　Itself for being there?
CAITHNESS　　　　　　Well, march we on
　To give obedience where 'tis truly owed.
　Meet we the medicine of the sickly weal,   27
　And with him pour we in our country's purge   28
　Each drop of us.
LENNOX　　　　　　Or so much as it needs   29
　To dew the sovereign flower and drown the weeds.   30
　Make we our march towards Birnam.

　　　　　　　　　　　　　　Exeunt, marching.

❖

5.3　*Enter Macbeth, Doctor, and attendants.*

MACBETH
　Bring me no more reports. Let them fly all!   1
　Till Birnam Wood remove to Dunsinane,

15 distempered disease-swollen, dropsical　**18 minutely** every minute.
upbraid censure.　**faith-breach** violation of all trust and sacred vows
19 in command under orders　**23 pestered** troubled, tormented
27 Meet we . . . weal i.e., let us join forces with Malcolm, the physician
of our sick land　**28–29 pour . . . of us** i.e., let us shed all our blood as a
bloodletting or *purge* of our country　**30 dew** bedew, water.　**sovereign**
(1) royal (2) medically efficacious

5.3. Location: Dunsinane. Macbeth's castle.
1 them i.e., the thanes.　**fly** desert

I cannot taint with fear. What's the boy Malcolm?   3
Was he not born of woman? The spirits that know
All mortal consequences have pronounced me thus: 5
"Fear not, Macbeth. No man that's born of woman
Shall e'er have power upon thee." Then fly, false thanes,
And mingle with the English epicures!   8
The mind I sway by and the heart I bear   9
Shall never sag with doubt nor shake with fear.   10

Enter Servant.

The devil damn thee black, thou cream-faced loon!   11
Where gott'st thou that goose look?

SERVANT
There is ten thousand—

MACBETH   Geese, villain?

SERVANT   Soldiers, sir.

MACBETH
Go prick thy face and over-red thy fear,   14
Thou lily-livered boy. What soldiers, patch?   15
Death of thy soul! Those linen cheeks of thine   16
Are counselors to fear. What soldiers, whey-face?   17

SERVANT   The English force, so please you.

MACBETH
Take thy face hence. [*Exit Servant.*] Seyton!—I am sick
   at heart
When I behold—Seyton, I say!—This push   20
Will cheer me ever, or disseat me now.   21
I have lived long enough. My way of life   22
Is fall'n into the sere, the yellow leaf,   23
And that which should accompany old age,
As honor, love, obedience, troops of friends,   25
I must not look to have, but in their stead

---

3 taint with become imbued or infected with, weakened by   **5 mortal consequences** what befalls humanity   **8 epicures** luxury-loving persons   **9 sway** rule myself   **10 sag** droop   **11 loon** stupid fellow   **14 Go prick . . . fear** i.e., go prick or pinch your pale cheeks to bring some color into them. (The servant's blood has all retired into his lower abdomen on account of his fear, so that he is very pale and there is no blood in his liver, where his courage should have resided—hence, *lily-livered* l. 15.)   **15 patch** domestic fool   **16 of thy** on your   **17 Are . . . fear** i.e., teach others to fear   **20 behold** (Macbeth does not finish this thought.)   **push** effort, crisis   **21 disseat** dethrone   **22 way** course   **23 sere** dry and withered   **25 As** such as

Curses, not loud but deep, mouth-honor, breath,
Which the poor heart would fain deny and dare not.
Seyton!

Enter Seyton.

SEYTON
What's your gracious pleasure?
MACBETH   What news more?
SEYTON
All is confirmed, my lord, which was reported.
MACBETH
I'll fight till from my bones my flesh be hacked.
Give me my armor.
SEYTON   'Tis not needed yet.
MACBETH   I'll put it on.
Send out more horses. Skirr the country round.   36
Hang those that talk of fear. Give me mine armor.
How does your patient, Doctor?
DOCTOR   Not so sick, my lord,
As she is troubled with thick-coming fancies
That keep her from her rest.
MACBETH   Cure her of that.
Canst thou not minister to a mind diseased,
Pluck from the memory a rooted sorrow,
Rase out the written troubles of the brain,   44
And with some sweet oblivious antidote   45
Cleanse the stuffed bosom of that perilous stuff   46
Which weighs upon the heart?
DOCTOR   Therein the patient
Must minister to himself.
MACBETH
Throw physic to the dogs! I'll none of it.   49
Come, put mine armor on. Give me my staff.   50
                  [*Attendants arm him.*]
Seyton, send out. Doctor, the thanes fly from me.—
Come, sir, dispatch.—If thou couldst, Doctor, cast   52
The water of my land, find her disease,   53

36 Skirr scour   **44 Rase** erase, obliterate. **written troubles of** troubles
written on   **45 oblivious** causing forgetfulness   **46 stuffed** clogged
49 physic medicine   **50 staff** lance or baton of office   **52 dispatch**
hurry. **cast** diagnose   **53 water** i.e., urine, used in diagnosis

And purge it to a sound and pristine health,
I would applaud thee to the very echo,
That should applaud again.—Pull 't off, I say.—   56
What rhubarb, senna, or what purgative drug   57
Would scour these English hence? Hear'st thou of
    them?   58

DOCTOR
Ay, my good lord. Your royal preparation
Makes us hear something.

MACBETH   Bring it after me.—   60
I will not be afraid of death and bane,
Till Birnam Forest come to Dunsinane.

                     Exeunt [all but the Doctor].

DOCTOR
Were I from Dunsinane away and clear,
Profit again should hardly draw me here.   [*Exit.*]

❖

5.4   *Drum and colors. Enter Malcolm, Siward,*
        Macduff, Siward's Son, Menteith, Caithness,
        Angus, [Lennox, Ross,] and soldiers, marching.

MALCOLM
Cousins, I hope the days are near at hand
That chambers will be safe.

MENTEITH   We doubt it nothing.   2

SIWARD
What wood is this before us?

MENTEITH   The wood of Birnam.

MALCOLM
Let every soldier hew him down a bough
And bear 't before him. Thereby shall we shadow
The numbers of our host and make discovery   6
Err in report of us.

SOLDIERS   It shall be done.

---

56 Pull 't off (Refers to some part of the armor not properly put on.)
57 senna a purgative drug   **58 scour** purge, cleanse, rid   **60 it** i.e., the
armor not yet put on Macbeth

5.4. Location: Country near Birnam Wood.
2 chambers . . . safe i.e., we may sleep safely in our bedchambers.
nothing not at all   **6 discovery** scouting reports

SIWARD
  We learn no other but the confident tyrant
  Keeps still in Dunsinane and will endure   9
  Our setting down before 't.
MALCOLM   'Tis his main hope;   10
  For where there is advantage to be given,   11
  Both more and less have given him the revolt,   12
  And none serve with him but constrainèd things
  Whose hearts are absent too.
MACDUFF   Let our just censures   14
  Attend the true event, and put we on   15
  Industrious soldiership.
SIWARD   The time approaches
  That will with due decision make us know
  What we shall say we have and what we owe.   18
  Thoughts speculative their unsure hopes relate,   19
  But certain issue strokes must arbitrate—   20
  Towards which advance the war.   *Exeunt, marching.*   21

❖

5.5   *Enter Macbeth, Seyton, and soldiers, with
            drum and colors.*

MACBETH
  Hang out our banners on the outward walls.
  The cry is still, "They come!" Our castle's strength
  Will laugh a siege to scorn. Here let them lie

9 Keeps remains. **endure** allow, not attempt to prevent   **10 setting
down before** laying siege to   **11 advantage** opportunity (i.e., in military
operations outside Macbeth's castle in which it is possible for would-be
deserters to slip away; in a siege, his forces will be more confined to the
castle and under his watchful eye)   **12 more and less** high and low
14–15 Let . . . event i.e., let us postpone judgment about these uncertain
matters until we've achieved our goal   **18 What . . . owe** i.e., what we
only claim to have, as distinguished from what we actually have (or
perhaps what we *owe* as duty).   **owe** own   **19–20 Thoughts . . . arbitrate** i.e., speculating can only convey our sense of hope; blows must
decide the actual outcome   **21 war** army

5.5. Location: Dunsinane. Macbeth's castle.

Till famine and the ague eat them up.
Were they not forced with those that should be ours,   5
We might have met them dareful, beard to beard,   6
And beat them backward home.

               A cry within of women.
               What is that noise?

SEYTON
  It is the cry of women, my good lord.
               [*He goes to the door.*]

MACBETH
  I have almost forgot the taste of fears.
  The time has been my senses would have cooled   10
  To hear a night-shriek, and my fell of hair   11
  Would at a dismal treatise rouse and stir   12
  As life were in 't. I have supped full with horrors;   13
  Direness, familiar to my slaughterous thoughts,
  Cannot once start me.

    [*Seyton returns.*]

               Wherefore was that cry?   15
SEYTON   The Queen, my lord, is dead.
MACBETH   She should have died hereafter;   17
  There would have been a time for such a word.
  Tomorrow, and tomorrow, and tomorrow   19
  Creeps in this petty pace from day to day
  To the last syllable of recorded time,   21
  And all our yesterdays have lighted fools
  The way to dusty death. Out, out, brief candle!   23
  Life's but a walking shadow, a poor player
  That struts and frets his hour upon the stage
  And then is heard no more. It is a tale
  Told by an idiot, full of sound and fury,
  Signifying nothing.   28

---

5 forced reinforced   **6 dareful** boldly, in open battle   **10 cooled** felt the chill of terror   **11 my fell of hair** the hair of my scalp   **12 dismal treatise** sinister story   **13 As** as if   **15 start me** make me start   **17 She . . . hereafter** she would have died someday; or, she should have died at some more appropriate time freed from the relentless pressures of the moment   **19–28 Tomorrow . . . nothing** (For biblical echoes in this speech, see Psalms 18:28, 22:15, 90:9; Job 8:9, 14:1–2, 18:6.)   **21 recorded time** the record of time   **23 dusty** (Since life, made out of dust, returns to dust.)

Enter a Messenger.

Thou com'st to use thy tongue; thy story quickly.
MESSENGER   Gracious my lord,
  I should report that which I say I saw,
  But know not how to do 't.
MACBETH   Well, say, sir.
MESSENGER
  As I did stand my watch upon the hill,
  I looked toward Birnam, and anon, methought,
  The wood began to move.
MACBETH   Liar and slave!
MESSENGER
  Let me endure your wrath if 't be not so.
  Within this three mile may you see it coming;
  I say, a moving grove.
MACBETH   If thou speak'st false,
  Upon the next tree shall thou hang alive
  Till famine cling thee. If thy speech be sooth,   40
  I care not if thou dost for me as much.
  I pull in resolution, and begin   42
  To doubt th' equivocation of the fiend
  That lies like truth. "Fear not, till Birnam Wood
  Do come to Dunsinane," and now a wood
  Comes toward Dunsinane. Arm, arm, and out!
  If this which he avouches does appear,
  There is nor flying hence nor tarrying here.
  I 'gin to be aweary of the sun,
  And wish th' estate o' the world were now undone.   50
  Ring the alarum bell! Blow wind, come wrack,   51
  At least we'll die with harness on our back.   *Exeunt.* 52

✢

5.6   *Drum and colors. Enter Malcolm, Siward,*
          Macduff, and their army, with boughs.

MALCOLM
  Now near enough. Your leafy screens throw down,

40 **cling** cause to shrivel.   **sooth** truth   42 **pull in** check, rein in
50 **estate** settled order   51 **wrack** ruin   52 **harness** armor
5.6. Location: Dunsinane. Before Macbeth's castle.

And show like those you are. You, worthy uncle,   2
Shall with my cousin, your right noble son,
Lead our first battle. Worthy Macduff and we   4
Shall take upon 's what else remains to do,
According to our order.
SIWARD   Fare you well.   6
Do we but find the tyrant's power tonight,   7
Let us be beaten if we cannot fight.

MACDUFF
Make all our trumpets speak! Give them all breath,
Those clamorous harbingers of blood and death.   10

            Exeunt. Alarums continued.

5.7   *Enter Macbeth.*

MACBETH
They have tied me to a stake. I cannot fly,
But bearlike I must fight the course. What's he   2
That was not born of woman? Such a one
Am I to fear, or none.

     Enter young Siward.

YOUNG SIWARD   What is thy name?
MACBETH   Thou'lt be afraid to hear it.
YOUNG SIWARD
No, though thou call'st thyself a hotter name
Than any is in hell.
MACBETH   My name's Macbeth.
YOUNG SIWARD
The devil himself could not pronounce a title
More hateful to mine ear.
MACBETH   No, nor more fearful.
YOUNG SIWARD
Thou liest, abhorrèd tyrant! With my sword

---

2 show appear   **4 battle** battalion   **6 order** plan of battle   **7 power**
army   **10 harbingers** forerunners

**5.7. Location: Before Macbeth's castle; the battle action is continuous
here.**
2 course bout or round of bearbaiting, in which the bear was tied to a
stake and dogs were set upon him

I'll prove the lie thou speak'st.
                    Fight, and young Siward slain.
MACBETH   Thou wast born of woman.   12
But swords I smile at, weapons laugh to scorn,
Brandished by man that's of a woman born.   *Exit.*

Alarums. Enter Macduff.

MACDUFF
That way the noise is. Tyrant, show thy face!
If thou be'st slain, and with no stroke of mine,
My wife and children's ghosts will haunt me still.
I cannot strike at wretched kerns, whose arms   18
Are hired to bear their staves. Either thou, Macbeth,   19
Or else my sword with an unbattered edge
I sheathe again undeeded. There thou shouldst be;   21
By this great clatter one of greatest note
Seems bruited. Let me find him, Fortune,   23
And more I beg not.   *Exit. Alarums.*

Enter Malcolm and Siward.

SIWARD
This way, my lord. The castle's gently rendered: 25
The tyrant's people on both sides do fight,
The noble thanes do bravely in the war,
The day almost itself professes yours,
And little is to do.
MALCOLM   We have met with foes
That strike beside us.
SIWARD   Enter, sir, the castle.   30
                    Exeunt. Alarum.

---

12 s.d. young Siward slain (In some unspecified way, young Siward's
body must be removed from the stage; his own father enters at l. 24 and
perceives nothing amiss, and in 5.8.38 young Siward is reported *missing*
in action. Perhaps Macbeth drags off the body, or perhaps it is removed
by soldiers during the alarums.)   **18 kerns** (Properly, Irish foot soldiers;
here applied contemptuously to the rank and file.)   **19 staves** spears.
Either thou i.e., either I find you   **21 undeeded** having seen no action
23 bruited announced   **25 rendered** surrendered   **30 strike beside us**
fight on our side, or miss us deliberately

5.8   *Enter Macbeth.*

MACBETH
Why should I play the Roman fool and die   1
On mine own sword? Whiles I see lives, the gashes   2
Do better upon them.

     Enter Macduff.

MACDUFF   Turn, hellhound, turn!
MACBETH
Of all men else I have avoided thee.
But get thee back. My soul is too much charged
With blood of thine already.
MACDUFF   I have no words;
My voice is in my sword, thou bloodier villain
Than terms can give thee out!   *Fight. Alarum.*
MACBETH   Thou losest labor.   8
As easy mayst thou the intrenchant air   9
With thy keen sword impress as make me bleed.   10
Let fall thy blade on vulnerable crests;
I bear a charmèd life, which must not yield
To one of woman born.
MACDUFF   Despair thy charm,   13
And let the angel whom thou still hast served   14
Tell thee, Macduff was from his mother's womb
Untimely ripped.   16
MACBETH
Accursèd be that tongue that tells me so,
For it hath cowed my better part of man!   18
And be these juggling fiends no more believed   19
That palter with us in a double sense,   20
That keep the word of promise to our ear
And break it to our hope. I'll not fight with thee.

5.8. **Location:** Before Macbeth's castle, as the battle continues; after
l. 34, within the castle.
1 Roman fool i.e., suicide, like Brutus, Mark Antony, and others
2 Whiles . . . lives i.e., as long as I see any enemy living   **8 give thee out**
name you, describe you   **9 intrenchant** that cannot be cut, indivisible
10 impress make an impression on   **13 Despair** despair of   **14 angel**
evil angel, Macbeth's genius. **still** always   **16 Untimely** prematurely
18 better . . . man i.e., courage   **19 juggling** deceiving   **20 palter . . .**
sense equivocate with us

MACDUFF   Then yield thee, coward,
And live to be the show and gaze o' the time!
We'll have thee, as our rarer monsters are,
Painted upon a pole, and underwrit,   26
"Here may you see the tyrant."
MACBETH   I will not yield
To kiss the ground before young Malcolm's feet
And to be baited with the rabble's curse.
Though Birnam Wood be come to Dunsinane,
And thou opposed, being of no woman born,
Yet I will try the last. Before my body   32
I throw my warlike shield. Lay on, Macduff,
And damned be him that first cries, "Hold, enough!"   34
                        Exeunt, fighting. Alarums.

> *Enter fighting, and Macbeth slain. [Exit Macduff*
> *with Macbeth's body.] Retreat, and flourish.*
> *Enter, with drum and colors, Malcolm, Siward,*
> *Ross, thanes, and soldiers.*

MALCOLM
I would the friends we miss were safe arrived.
SIWARD
Some must go off; and yet, by these I see   36
So great a day as this is cheaply bought.
MALCOLM
Macduff is missing, and your noble son.
ROSS
Your son, my lord, has paid a soldier's debt.
He only lived but till he was a man,
The which no sooner had his prowess confirmed
In the unshrinking station where he fought,   42
But like a man he died.
SIWARD   Then he is dead?

---

26 Painted . . . pole i.e., painted on a board suspended on a pole   **32 the
last** i.e., my last resort: my own strength and resolution   **34 s.d. Enter,
with drum and colors, etc.** (The remainder of the play is perhaps imagined as taking place in Macbeth's castle, and could be marked as a
separate scene. In Shakespeare's theater, however, the shift is so nonrepresentational and without scenic alteration that the action is virtually
continuous.)   **36 go off** die.   **by these** to judge by these (assembled)
42 unshrinking station post from which he did not shrink

ROSS
Ay, and brought off the field. Your cause of sorrow
Must not be measured by his worth, for then
It hath no end.

SIWARD   Had he his hurts before?

ROSS
Ay, on the front.

SIWARD   Why then, God's soldier be he!
Had I as many sons as I have hairs
I would not wish them to a fairer death.
And so, his knell is knolled.

MALCOLM   He's worth more sorrow,
And that I'll spend for him.

SIWARD   He's worth no more.
They say he parted well and paid his score,   52
And so, God be with him! Here comes newer comfort.

     Enter Macduff, with Macbeth's head.

MACDUFF
Hail, King! For so thou art. Behold where stands   54
Th' usurper's cursèd head. The time is free.   55
I see thee compassed with thy kingdom's pearl,   56
That speak my salutation in their minds,
Whose voices I desire aloud with mine:
Hail, King of Scotland!

ALL   Hail, King of Scotland!   *Flourish.*

MALCOLM
We shall not spend a large expense of time
Before we reckon with your several loves   62
And make us even with you. My thanes and kinsmen,   63
Henceforth be earls, the first that ever Scotland
In such an honor named. What's more to do
Which would be planted newly with the time,   66
As calling home our exiled friends abroad
That fled the snares of watchful tyranny,

---

52 parted departed.   **score** reckoning   **54 stands** i.e., on a pole   **55 free** released from tyranny   **56 compassed . . . pearl** surrounded by the nobles of your kingdom (literally, the pearls encircling a crown) **62 reckon** come to a reckoning   **63 make . . . you** i.e., repay your worthiness   **66 would . . . time** i.e., should be established at the commencement of this new era

Producing forth the cruel ministers   69
Of this dead butcher and his fiendlike queen—
Who, as 'tis thought, by self and violent hands   71
Took off her life—this, and what needful else
That calls upon us, by the grace of Grace
We will perform in measure, time, and place.
So, thanks to all at once and to each one,
Whom we invite to see us crowned at Scone.
                             Flourish. Exeunt omnes.

69 Producing forth bringing forward to trial.   **ministers** agents
71 self and violent her own violent

Date and Text

Macbeth was first printed in the First Folio of 1623. It was set up from a promptbook or a transcript of one. The text is unusually short, and seems to have been cut for reasons of censorship or for some special performance. Moreover, all of 3.5 and parts of 4.1 (39–43, 125–132) appear to be interpolations, containing songs from Thomas Middleton's *The Witch*. Middleton may have been responsible for other alterations and additions.

An astrologer named Simon Forman, in his manuscript *The Book of Plays and Notes thereof per Formans for Common Policy*, records the first known performance of *Macbeth* on April 20, 1611, at the Globe Theatre. The play must have been in existence by 1607, however, for allusions to it seemingly occur in *Lingua* and *The Puritan* (both published in 1607) and in *The Knight of the Burning Pestle* (probably acted in 1607). On the other hand, the play itself seemingly alludes to James I's royal succession in 1603, and to the trial of the notorious Gunpowder Plot conspirators in March of 1606.

Textual Notes

These textual notes are not a historical collation, either of the early folios or of more recent editions; they are simply a record of departures in this edition from the copy text. The reading adopted in this edition appears in boldface, followed by the rejected reading from the copy text, i.e., the First Folio. Only major alterations in punctuation are noted. Changes in lineation are not indicated, nor are some minor and obvious typographical errors.

Abbreviations used:
F the First Folio
s.d. stage direction
s.p. speech prefix

Copy text: the First Folio

1.1. 9 s.p. Second Witch All   **10 s.p. Third Witch** [not in F]   **11 s.p. All** [at l. 9 in F]

1.2. 1 s.p. [and elsewhere] Duncan King   **13 gallowglasses** Gallowgrosses   **14 quarrel** Quarry   **21 ne'er** neu'r   **26 thunders break** Thunders

1.3. 32 Weird weyward [elsewhere in F spelled "weyward" or "weyard"]   **39 Forres** Soris   **98 Came** Can   **111 lose** loose

1.4. 1 Are Or

1.5. 1 s.p. [and elsewhere] Lady Macbeth Lady   **12 lose** loose   **47 it** hit

1.6. 4 martlet Barlet   **9 most** must

1.7. 6 shoal Schoole   **48 do** no

2.1. 56 strides sides   **57 sure** sowre   **58 way they** they may

2.2. 13 s.d. [at l. 8 in F]

2.3. 41 s.d. [at l. 40 in F]

3.1. 76 s.p. Murderers Murth [also at ll. 116 and 141]   **142 s.d. Exeunt** [after l. 143 in F]

3.3. 7 and end

3.4. 79 time times   **122 s.d. Exeunt** Exit

3.6. 24 son Sonnes   **38 the** their

4.1. 34 ingredients ingredience   **38 s.d. to** and   **59 germens** Germaine   **93 Dunsinane** Dunsmane   **94 s.d. Descends** Descend   **98 Birnam** Byrnam [also spelled "Byrnam" at l. 93 and "Birnan," "Byrnane," and "Birnane" in Act 5]   **119 eighth** eight

4.2. 1 s.p. [and throughout] Lady Macduff Wife   **22 none** moue   **70–71 ones . . . methinks** ones / To fright you thus. Me thinks   **80 s.d. Enter Murderers** [after "What are these faces" in F]   **81 s.p. [and throughout scene] First Murderer** Mur   **84 shag-haired** shagge-ear'd

4.3. 4 downfall'n downfall   **15 deserve** discerne   **35 Fare** Far   **108 accursed** accust   **124 detraction, here** detraction. Heere   **134 thy** they   **237 tune** time

5.1. 37 fear who feare? who

5.3. 41 Cure her Cure   **54 pristine** pristiue   **57 senna** Cyme   **62 s.d.** [at l. 64 in F]

5.4. 16 s.p. Siward Sey

Shakespeare's Sources

Shakespeare's chief source for *Macbeth* was Raphael Holinshed's *Chronicles* (1587 edition). Holinshed had gone for most of his material to Hector Boece, *Scotorum Historiae* (1526–1527), who in turn was indebted to a fourteenth-century priest named John of Fordun and to a fifteenth-century chronicler, Andrew of Wyntoun. By the time Holinshed found it, the story of Macbeth had become more fiction than fact. The historical Macbeth, who ruled from 1040 to 1057, did take the throne by killing Duncan, but in a civil conflict between two clans contending for the kingship. Contemporary observers credit him with having been a good ruler. Although he was defeated by the Earl of Northumbria (the Siward of Shakespeare's play) at Birnam Wood in 1054, the Earl was forced by his own losses to retire, and Macbeth ruled three years longer before being slain by Duncan's son Malcolm. Banquo and Fleance are fictional characters apparently invented by Boece.

In Holinshed's telling of the story, as we see in the selection that follows, Duncan is a king of a soft and gentle nature, negligent in punishing his enemies and thereby an unwitting encourager of sedition. It falls to his cousin, Macbeth, a critic of this soft line, and to Banquo, the Thane of Lochaber, to defend Scotland against her enemies: first against Macdowald (Macdonwald in Shakespeare) with his Irish kerns and gallowglasses, and then against Sueno, King of Norway. (Shakespeare fuses these battles into one.) Shortly thereafter, Macbeth and Banquo encounter "three women in strange and wild apparel, resembling creatures of elder world," who predict their futures as in the play. Although Macbeth and Banquo jest about the matter, common opinion later maintains that "these women were either the Weird Sisters, that is (as ye would say), the goddesses of destiny, or else some nymphs or fairies endued with knowledge of prophecy." Certainly Macbeth soon becomes the Thane of Cawdor, whereupon, jestingly reminded of the three sisters' promise by Banquo, he resolves to seek the throne. His way is blocked, however, by Duncan's naming of his eldest but still underage son

Malcolm to be Prince of Cumberland and heir to the throne.
Macbeth's resentment at this is understandable, since Scottish law provides that, until the King's son is of age, the
"next of blood unto him"—i.e., Macbeth himself, as Duncan's cousin—should reign. Accordingly, Macbeth begins to
plot with his associates how to usurp the kingdom by force.
His "very ambitious" wife urges him on because of her
"unquenchable desire" to be queen. Banquo is one among
many trusted friends with whose support Macbeth slays
the King at Inverness or at Bothgowanan. (No mention is
made of a visit to Macbeth's castle.) Malcolm and Donald
Bane, the dead King's sons, fly for their safety to Cumberland, where Malcolm is well received by Edward the
Confessor of England; Donald Bane proceeds on to Ireland.

  Holinshed's Macbeth is at first no brutal tyrant, as in
Shakespeare. For some ten years he rules well, using great
liberality and correcting the laxity of his predecessor's
reign. (Holinshed does suggest, to be sure, that his justice is
only contrived to court popularity among his subjects.) Inevitably, however, the Weird Sisters' promise of a posterity
to Banquo goads Macbeth into ordering the murder of his
onetime companion. Fleance escapes Macbeth's henchmen
in the dark, and afterward founds the lineage of the Stuart
kings. (This genealogy is fictitious.) Macbeth's vain quest
for absolute power further causes him to build Dunsinane
fortress. When Macduff refuses to help, the King turns
against him and would kill him except that "a certain
witch, whom he had in great trust," tells the King he need
never fear a man born of woman nor any vanquishment till
Birnam Wood come to Dunsinane. Macduff flees for his
safety into England and joins Malcolm, whereupon Macbeth's agents slaughter Macduff's wife and children at Fife.
Malcolm, fearing that Macduff may be an agent of Macbeth,
dissemblingly professes to be a voluptuary, miser, and tyrant; but when Macduff responds as he should in righteous
sorrow at Scotland's evil condition, Malcolm reveals his
steadfast commitment to the cause of right. These leaders
return to Scotland and defeat Macbeth at Birnam Wood,
with their soldiers carrying branches before them. Macduff, proclaiming that he is a man born of no woman since
he was "ripped out" of his mother's womb, slays Macbeth.

Despite extensive similarities, Shakespeare has made some significant changes. Duncan is no longer an ineffectual king. Macbeth can no longer justify his claim to the throne. Most important, Banquo is no longer partner to a broadly based though secret conspiracy against Duncan. Banquo is, after all, ancestor of James I (at least according to this legendary history), so that his hands must be kept scrupulously clean; King James disapproved of all tyrannicides, whatever the circumstances. Macbeth is no longer a just lawgiver. The return of Banquo's ghost to Macbeth's banqueting table is an added scene. Macbeth hears the prophecy about Birnam Wood and Macduff from the Weird Sisters, not, as in Holinshed, from some witch. Lady Macbeth's role is considerably enhanced, and her sleepwalking scene is original. Shakespeare compresses time, as he usually does.

In making some of these alterations, Shakespeare turned to another story in Holinshed's chronicle of Scotland: the murder of King Duff by Donwald (historically preceding the chronicle of Duncan in the following pages). King Duff, never suspecting any treachery in Donwald, often spends time at the castle of Forres, where Donwald is captain of the castle. On one occasion Donwald's wife, bearing great malice toward the King, shows Donwald (who already bears a grudge against Duff) "the means whereby he might soonest accomplish" the murder. The husband and wife ply Duff's few chamberlains with much to eat and drink. Donwald abhors the act "greatly in heart," but perseveres "through instigation of his wife." Four of Donwald's servants actually commit the murder under his instruction. Next morning, Donwald breaks into the King's chamber and slays the chamberlains as though believing them guilty. Donwald is so overzealous in his investigation of the murder that many lords begin to suspect him of having done it. For six months afterward, the sun refuses to appear by day and the moon by night.

The chronicle accounts in Holinshed of Malcolm and Edward the Confessor supplied Shakespeare with further details. A more important supplementary source may have been George Buchanan's *Rerum Scoticarum Historia* (1582), a Latin history not translated in Shakespeare's lifetime, presenting a more complex psychological portrait of the protagonist than in Holinshed. Finally, Shakespeare may have known King James I's *Daemonology* (1597), John Studley's early seventeenth-century version of Seneca's *Medea*, Samuel Harsnett's *Declaration of Egregious Popish Impostures* (1603), and accounts of the Scottish witch trials published around 1590.

The First and Second Volumes
of Chronicles (1587 edition)
Compiled by Raphael Holinshed

VOLUME 2: THE HISTORY OF SCOTLAND

DUFF

[King Duff of Scotland, having been restored to health from
a sickness in which the magical practice of witches is said
to have played a part, undertakes a campaign into Moray-
land against the rebels there. He apprehends them and
brings them back to the royal castle at Forres to be hanged
as traitors.]

Amongst them there were also certain young gentlemen,
right beautiful and goodly personages, being near of kin
unto Donwald, captain of the castle, and had been per-
suaded to be partakers with the other rebels more through
the fraudulent counsel of divers wicked persons than of
their own accord. Whereupon the foresaid Donwald, la-
menting their case, made earnest labor and suit to the King
to have begged their pardon; but having a plain denial, he
conceived such an inward malice towards the King (though
he showed it not outwardly at the first) that the same continued still boiling in his stomach[1] and ceased not till,
through setting on of his wife and in revenge of such
unthankfulness, he found means to murder the King within
the foresaid castle of Forres where he used to sojourn. For
the King, being in that country, was accustomed to lie most
commonly within the same castle, having a special trust in
Donwald as a man whom he never suspected.

But Donwald, not forgetting the reproach which his lineage[2] had sustained by the execution of those his kinsmen
whom the King for a spectacle to the people had caused to
be hanged, could not but show manifest tokens of great
grief at home amongst his family, which his wife, perceiving, ceased not to travail[3] with him till she understood what

1 **stomach** i.e., bosom, innermost thoughts   2 **lineage** family   3 **travail**
labor, strive

the cause was of his displeasure. Which at length when she
had learned by his own relation, she, as one that bare no
less malice in her heart towards the King for the like cause
on her behalf than her husband did for his friends', counseled him (sith[4] the King oftentimes used to lodge in his
house without any guard about him other than the garrison
of the castle, which was wholly at his[5] commandment) to
make him away, and showed him the means whereby he
might soonest accomplish it.

Donwald, thus being the more kindled in wrath by the
words of his wife, determined to follow her advice in the
execution of so heinous an act. Whereupon, devising with
himself for a while which way he might best accomplish his
cursed intent, at length gat[6] opportunity and sped his purpose as followeth. It chanced that the King, upon the day
before he purposed to depart forth of the castle, was long in
his oratory[7] at his prayers and there continued till it was
late in the night. At the last, coming forth, he called such
afore him[8] as had faithfully served him in pursuit and ap-
prehension of the rebels, and, giving them hearty thanks, he
bestowed sundry honorable gifts amongst them, of the
which number Donwald was one, as he that had been ever
accounted a most faithful servant to the King.

At length, having talked with them a long time, he got
him[9] into his privy chamber only with two of his chamberlains who, having brought him to bed, came forth again and
then fell to banqueting with Donwald and his wife, who had
prepared divers delicate dishes and sundry sorts of drinks
for their rear supper or collation;[10] whereat they sat up so
long till they had charged their stomachs with such full
gorges[11] that their heads were no sooner got to the pillow
but asleep they were so fast that a man might have removed
the chamber over them sooner than to have awaked them
out of their drunken sleep.

Then Donwald, though he abhorred the act greatly in
heart, yet through instigation of his wife he called four of
his servants unto him whom he had made privy to his

---

4 sith since   **5 his** i.e., Donwald's, as captain of the castle   **6 gat** i.e., he
got   **7 oratory** small chapel   **8 such afore him** such persons before him
9 got him betook himself   **10 rear supper or collation** repast at the end
of the day   **11 such full gorges** i.e., so much food

wicked intent before and framed[12] to his purpose with large gifts. And now declaring[13] unto them after what sort they should work the feat, they gladly obeyed his instructions, and speedily going about the murder they entered* the chamber in which the King lay a little before cock's crow,[14] where they secretly cut his throat as he lay sleeping, without any buskling at all. And immediately, by a postern[15] gate, they carried forth the dead body into the fields, and, throwing it upon an horse there provided ready for that purpose, they conveyed* it unto a place about two miles distant from the castle, where they stayed and gat certain laborers to help them to turn the course of a little river running through the fields there; and digging a deep hole in the channel, they buried* the body in the same, ramming it up with stones and gravel so closely that, setting the water in the right course again, no man could perceive that anything had been newly digged there. This they did by order appointed them by Donwald (as is reported), for that[16] the body should not be found and, by bleeding when Donwald should be present, declare him to be guilty of the murder. For such an opinion men have that the dead corpse of any man, being slain, will bleed abundantly if the murderer be present. But for what consideration soever they buried him there, they had no sooner finished the work but that they slew them whose help they used herein, and straightways thereupon fled into Orkney.

Donwald, about the time that the murder was in doing,[17] got him amongst them that kept the watch[18] and so continued in company with them all the residue of the night. But in the morning, when the noise was raised in the King's chamber how the King was slain, his body conveyed away, and the bed all berayed[19] with blood, he with the watch ran thither as though he had known nothing of the matter and, breaking into the chamber and finding cakes[20] of blood in the bed and on the floor about the sides of it, he forthwith

---

12 framed shaped, inclined   **13 And now declaring** i.e., and he now declaring   **14 cock's crow** (The first cock supposedly crowed at midnight.)   **15 buskling . . . postern** scuffling . . . back, private   **16 for that** in order that   **17 in doing** being done   **18 amongst . . . watch** among those who were standing watch. (Donwald's reason for doing so is to have an alibi.)   **19 berayed** befouled   **20 cakes** clots

slew the chamberlains as guilty of that heinous murder.
And then, like a madman, running to and fro, he ransacked
every corner within the castle as though it had been to have
seen if he might have found either the body or any of the
murderers hid in any privy place. But at length coming to
the postern gate and finding it open, he burdened the chamberlains whom he had slain with all the fault, they having
the keys of the gates committed to their keeping all the
night, and therefore it could not be otherwise (said he) but
that they were of counsel in the committing of that most
detestable murder.

Finally, such was his overearnest diligence in the severe
inquisition and trial of the offenders herein that some of
the lords began to mislike the matter and to smell forth
shrewd tokens[21] that he should not be altogether clear himself. But forsomuch as they were in that country where he
had the whole rule, what by reason of[22] his friends and authority together, they doubted[23] to utter what they thought
till time and place should better serve thereunto, and hereupon got them away, every man to his home. For the space
of six months together after this heinous murder thus committed, there appeared no sun by day nor moon by night in
any part of the realm, but still[24] was the sky covered with
continual clouds, and sometimes such outrageous winds
arose, with lightnings and tempests, that the people were in
great fear of present destruction. . . .

Monstrous sights also that were seen within the Scottish
kingdom that year were these: Horses in Lothian, being of
singular beauty and swiftness, did eat their own flesh and
would in no wise taste any other meat.[25] In Angus there was
a gentlewoman brought forth a child without eyes, nose,
hand, or foot. There was a sparhawk[26] also strangled by
an owl. Neither was it any less wonder that the sun, as before is said, was continually covered with clouds for six
months' space. But all men understood that the abominable murder of King Duff was the cause hereof, which being
revenged by the death of the authors[27] (in manner as before

---

21 shrewd tokens malignant or ominous indications   **22 what by reason
of** i.e., what with   **23 doubted** feared   **24 still** continually   **25 meat**
food   **26 sparhawk** sparrowhawk   **27 the authors** i.e., Duff's chamberlains, presumed guilty

is said), Cullen was crowned as lawful successor to the same Duff at Scone, with all due honor and solemnity, in the year of our Lord 972, after that Duff had ruled the Scottish kingdom about the space of four years.

[Kenneth, a brother of Duff, succeeds to the Scottish throne after Cullen is murdered by a thane whose daughter he has ravished. In order that his own sons might enjoy the crown, Kenneth poisons Malcolm, son of King Duff and presumed heir to the Scottish kingdom. Though no suspicion falls on Kenneth, he is so tormented by his conscience that he hears voices in the night assuring him that God knows his every secret. After a series of bloody civil wars, another Malcolm succeeds to the Scottish throne and rules for thirty-two years.]

Duncan

After Malcolm, succeeded his nephew[1] Duncan, the son of his daughter Beatrice. For Malcolm had two daughters. The one, which was this Beatrice, being given in marriage unto one Abbanath Crinen, a man of great nobility and thane of the Isles and west parts of Scotland, bare of that marriage the foresaid Duncan. The other, called Doada, was married unto Sinel, the Thane of Glamis, by whom she had issue one Macbeth, a valiant gentleman and one that, if he had not been somewhat cruel of nature, might have been thought most worthy the government of a realm. On the other part, Duncan was so soft and gentle of nature that the people wished the inclinations and manners of these two cousins to have been so tempered[2] and interchangeably bestowed betwixt them that, where the one had too much of clemency and the other of cruelty, the mean virtue betwixt these two extremities might have reigned by indifferent[3] partition in them both; so should Duncan have proved a worthy king and Macbeth an excellent captain. The beginning of Duncan's reign was very quiet and peaceable, without any notable trouble; but after it was perceived how negligent he was in punishing offenders, many misruled[4] persons took occa-

1 **nephew** i.e., grandson   2 **tempered** mixed, blended   3 **indifferent** evenhanded   4 **misruled** disorderly

sion thereof to trouble the peace and quiet state of the commonwealth by seditious commotions which first had their beginnings in this wise.

Banquo, the Thane of Lochaber, of whom the House of the Stuarts is descended, the which by order of lineage hath now for a long time enjoyed the crown of Scotland even till these our days, as he gathered the finances due to the King and further punished somewhat sharply such as were notorious offenders, being assailed by a number of rebels inhabiting in that country and spoiled[5] of the money and all other things, had much ado to get away with life after he had received sundry grievous wounds amongst them. Yet escaping their hands, after he was somewhat recovered of his hurts and was able to ride, he repaired[6] to the court, where, making his complaint to the King in most earnest wise, he purchased[7] at length that the offenders were sent for by a sergeant-at-arms to appear to make answer unto such matters as should be laid to their charge. But they, augmenting their mischievous act with a more wicked deed, after they had misused the messenger with sundry kinds of reproaches, they finally slew him also.

Then, doubting not but for such contemptuous demeanor against the King's regal authority they should be invaded with all the power the King could make, Macdowald, one of great estimation among them, making first a confederacy with his nearest friends and kinsmen, took upon him to be chief captain of all such rebels as would stand against the King in maintenance of their grievous offenses lately committed against him. Many slanderous words also and railing taunts this Macdowald uttered against his prince, calling him a fainthearted milksop more meet to govern a sort[8] of idle monks in some cloister than to have the rule of such valiant and hardy men-of-war as the Scots were. He used also such subtle persuasions and forged allurements that in a small time he had gotten together a mighty power[9] of men; for out of the Western Isles there came unto him a great multitude of people offering themselves to assist him in that rebellious quarrel, and out of Ireland in hope of the

5 **spoiled** plundered   6 **repaired** went, returned   7 **purchased** arranged, contrived   8 **sort** gang, bunch   9 **power** army

spoil[10] came no small number of kerns and gallowglasses,[11] offering gladly to serve under him whither[12] it should please him to lead them.

Macdowald, thus having a mighty puissance[13] about him, encountered with such of the King's people as were sent against him into Lochaber and, discomfiting them, by mere[14] force took their captain Malcolm and after the end of the battle smote off his head. This overthrow, being notified[15] to the King, did put him in wonderful[16] fear by reason of his small skill in warlike affairs. Calling therefore his nobles to a council, he asked of them their best advice for the subduing of Macdowald and other the rebels. Here in sundry heads (as ever it happeneth) were sundry opinions, which they uttered according to every man his skill. At length Macbeth, speaking much against the King's softness and overmuch slackness in punishing offenders, whereby they had such time to assemble together, he promised notwithstanding, if the charge were committed[17] unto him and unto Banquo, so to order the matter that the rebels should be shortly vanquished and quite put down, and that not so much as one of them should be found to make resistance within the country.

And even so it came to pass. For, being sent forth with a new power,[18] at his entering into Lochaber the fame of his coming put the enemies in such fear that a great number of them stale secretly away from their captain Macdowald, who nevertheless, enforced thereto, gave battle unto Macbeth with the residue which remained with him. But being overcome and fleeing for refuge into a castle (within the which his wife and children were enclosed), at length, when he saw how he could neither defend the hold[19] any longer against his enemies nor yet upon surrender be suffered to depart with life saved, he first slew his wife and children and lastly himself, lest if he had yielded simply he should have been executed in most cruel wise for an example to

---

10 **spoil** plunder   11 **kerns and gallowglasses** light-armed Irish foot soldiers and horsemen armed with axes   12 **whither** wherever 13 **puissance** power, military force   14 **discomfiting . . . mere** overthrowing . . . sheer   15 **notified** conveyed   16 **wonderful** great 17 **charge were committed** command were given   18 **power** army 19 **hold** stronghold, fortified place of defense

other.[20] Macbeth, entering into the castle by the gates as
then[21] set open, found the carcass of Macdowald lying dead
there amongst the residue of the slain bodies, which, when
he beheld, remitting no piece of his cruel nature with that
pitiful sight, he caused the head to be cut off and set upon a
pole's end, and so sent it as a present to the King, who as
then lay at Bertha.[22] The headless trunk he commanded to
be hung up upon an high pair of gallows.

[No sooner has order been restored by Macbeth than
Sueno, King of Norway, arrives in Fife "with a puissant
army to subdue the whole realm of Scotland." Sueno's
forces do well at first and besiege the Scots, but then let
down their guard in drunken rioting and are slaughtered by
Macbeth. Sueno flees. The Scots celebrate their notable victory with processions and offerings to God; but soon the
Danes, acting under the orders of Canute, King of England,
send another force to revenge the overthrow and subse-
quent death of Canute's brother, Sueno. Macbeth and Banquo, commissioned by King Duncan to meet this threat, act
with great success, overwhelming the Danes to such a de-
gree that the latter are constrained to pay Macbeth handsomely for the right to have their dead buried at Saint
Colme's Inch—i.e., Inchcolm, the Isle of St. Columba in the
Firth of Forth. Peace is concluded between the Scots and
the Danes.]

Shortly after happened a strange and uncouth[23] wonder,
which afterward was the cause of much trouble in the
realm of Scotland, as ye shall after hear. It fortuned, as
Macbeth and Banquo journeyed toward Forres where the
King then lay, they went sporting[24] by the way together
without other company save only themselves, passing
thorough the woods and fields, when suddenly, in the midst
of a laund,[25] there met them three women in strange and
wild apparel, resembling creatures of elder world,[26] whom
when they attentively beheld, wondering much at the sight,
the first of them spake and said, "All hail, Macbeth, Thane

20 other others   21 as then at that time   22 lay at Bertha resided at
Perth   23 uncouth unaccustomed   24 sporting for pleasure   25 laund
glade   26 elder world ancient times

of Glamis!" (for he had lately entered into that dignity and office by the death of his father Sinel). The second of them said, "Hail, Macbeth, Thane of Cawdor!" But the third said, "All hail, Macbeth, that hereafter shalt be King of Scotland!"

Then Banquo: "What manner of women," saith he, "are you, that seem so little favorable unto me, whereas to my fellow here, besides high offices, ye assign also the kingdom, appointing forth nothing for me at all?" "Yes," saith the first of them, "we promise greater benefits unto thee than unto him, for he shall reign indeed, but with an unlucky end, neither shall he leave any issue[27] behind him to succeed in his place; where, contrarily, thou indeed shalt not reign at all, but of thee those shall be born which shall govern the Scottish kingdom by long order of continual descent." Herewith the foresaid women vanished immediately out of their sight. This was reputed at the first but some vain fantastical illusion by Macbeth and Banquo, insomuch that Banquo would call Macbeth, in jest, King of Scotland, and Macbeth again would call him, in sport likewise, the father of many kings. But afterwards the common opinion was that these women were either the Weird Sisters, that is (as ye would say), the goddesses of destiny, or else some nymphs or fairies endued with knowledge of prophecy by their necromantical science, because everything came to pass as they had spoken. For shortly after, the Thane of Cawdor being condemned at Forres of treason against the King committed, his lands, livings, and offices were given of[28] the King's liberality to Macbeth.

The same night after, at supper, Banquo jested with him and said, "Now Macbeth, thou hast obtained those things which the two former sisters prophesied; there remaineth only for thee to purchase[29] that which the third said should come to pass." Whereupon Macbeth, revolving the thing in his mind, began even then to devise how he might attain to the kingdom. But yet he thought with himself that he must tarry a time which should advance him thereto by the divine providence, as it had come to pass in his former preferment.[30] But shortly after it chanced that King Duncan,

27 issue offspring   **28 of** through   **29 purchase** obtain   **30 preferment**
advancement

having two sons by his wife (which was the daughter of Siward, Earl of Northumberland), he made the elder of them,
called Malcolm, Prince of Cumberland, as it were thereby
to appoint him his successor in the kingdom immediately
after his decease. Macbeth, sore troubled herewith for that
he saw by this means his hope sore hindered (where, by the
old laws of the realm, the ordinance was that if he that
should succeed were not of able age to take the charge upon
himself, he that was next of blood unto him should be ad-
mitted), he began to take counsel how he might usurp the
kingdom by force, having a just quarrel[31] so to do, as he
took[32] the matter, for that Duncan did what in him lay[33] to
defraud him of all manner of title and claim which he
might, in time to come, pretend[34] unto the crown.

The words of the three Weird Sisters also (of whom before
ye have heard) greatly encouraged him hereunto; but spe-
cially his wife lay sore upon him[35] to attempt the thing, as
she that was very ambitious, burning in unquenchable desire to bear the name of a queen. At length, therefore, com-
municating his purposed intent with his trusty friends,
amongst whom Banquo was the chiefest, upon confidence
of their promised aid he slew the King at Inverness or (as
some say) at Bothgowanan, in the sixth year of his reign.
Then, having a company about him of such as he had made
privy to his enterprise, he caused himself to be proclaimed
king and forthwith went unto Scone, where by common
consent he received the investure[36] of the kingdom according to the accustomed manner. The body of Duncan was
first conveyed unto Elgin and there buried in kingly wise;
but afterwards it was removed and conveyed unto Colmekill
and there laid in a sepulture amongst his predecessors, in
the year after the birth of our Saviour 1046.

Malcolm Cammore and Donald Bane, the sons of King
Duncan, for fear of their lives (which they might well know
that Macbeth would seek to bring to end for his more sure
confirmation in the estate), fled into Cumberland, where
Malcolm remained till time that Saint Edward, the son of

---

31 quarrel cause, occasion   **32 took** understood   **33 for that . . . lay**
because Duncan did all that lay in his power   **34 pretend** lay claim
35 lay sore upon him pressed him hard, nagged at him   **36 investure**
investiture, ceremonial robes and symbols of rule

Ethelred, recovered the dominion of England from the Danish power; the which Edward received Malcolm by way of most friendly entertainment;[37] but Donald passed over into Ireland where he was tenderly cherished by the king of that land. Macbeth, after the departure thus of Duncan's sons, used great liberality towards the nobles of the realm, thereby to win their favor; and, when he saw that no man went about to trouble him, he set his whole intention to maintain justice and to punish all enormities and abuses which had chanced through the feeble and slothful administration of Duncan. . . . Macbeth, showing himself thus a most diligent punisher of all injuries and wrongs attempted by any disordered[38] persons within his realm, was accounted the sure defense and buckler[39] of innocent people; and hereto he also applied his whole endeavor to cause young men to exercise themselves in virtuous manners, and men of the Church to attend their divine service according to their vocations.

He caused to be slain sundry thanes, as of Caithness, Sutherland, Stranaverne, and Ross, because through them and their seditious attempts much trouble daily rose in the realm. He appeased the troubled state of Galloway, and slew one Magill, a tyrant who had many years before passed nothing of[40] the regal authority or power. To be brief, such were the worthy doings and princely acts of this Macbeth in the administration of the realm that if he had attained thereunto by rightful means and continued in uprightness of justice, as he began, till the end of his reign, he might well have been numbered amongst the most noble princes that anywhere had reigned. He made many wholesome laws and statutes for the public weal of his subjects.

[Holinshed here prints the laws made by King Macbeth, according to Hector Boece's *Scotoram Historiae*.]

These and the like commendable laws Macbeth caused to be put as then in use, governing the realm for the space of ten years in equal justice. But this was but a counterfeit zeal of equity showed by him, partly against his natural in-

---

37 by way of . . . entertainment with friendly reception **38 disordered** disorderly **39 buckler** shield **40 passed nothing of** paid no regard to

clination, to purchase thereby the favor of the people.
Shortly after, he began to show what he was, instead of equity practicing cruelty. For the prick of conscience (as it
chanceth[41] ever in tyrants and such as attain to any estate by
unrighteous means) caused him ever to fear lest he should
be served of the same cup as he had ministered to his predecessor. The words also of the three Weird Sisters would not
out of his mind, which,[42] as they promised him the kingdom, so likewise did they promise it at the same time unto
the posterity of Banquo. He willed therefore the same Banquo, with his son named Fleance, to come to a supper that
he had prepared for them; which was indeed, as he had devised, present[43] death at the hands of certain murderers
whom he hired to execute that deed, appointing[44] them to
meet with the same Banquo and his son without[45] the palace as they returned to their lodgings and there to slay
them, so that he would not have his house slandered,[46] but
that in time to come he might clear himself if anything were
laid to his charge upon any suspicion that might arise.

It chanced by the benefit of the dark night that, though
the father were slain, yet the son, by* the help of almighty
God reserving him to better fortune, escaped that danger;
and afterwards having some inkling, by the admonition of
some friends which he had in the court, how his life was
sought no less than his father's—who was slain not by
chance-medley,[47] as by the handling of the matter Macbeth
would have had it to appear, but even upon a prepensed[48]
device—whereupon to avoid further peril he fled into
Wales. But here I think it shall not much make against my
purpose if, according to the order which I find observed in
the Scottish history, I shall in few words rehearse[49] the original line of those kings which have descended from the foresaid Banquo, that they which have enjoyed the kingdom by
so long continuance of descent, from one to another and
that even unto these our days, may be known from whence
they had their first beginning.

---

41 chanceth happens   **42 which** who   **43 present** immediate   **44 appointing** arranging for   **45 without** outside of   **46 so that . . . slandered** i.e.,
so that his royal *house* or lineage should not suffer the reproach of having committed murder   **47 chance-medley** accidental homicide   **48 prepensed** premeditated   **49 rehearse** recite, name

[Holinshed here traces the line of descent from Fleance to James VI, King of Scotland in the late sixteenth century.]

But to return unto Macbeth in continuing the history, and to begin where I left, ye shall understand that after the contrived slaughter of Banquo, nothing prospered with the foresaid Macbeth. For in manner[50] every man began to doubt[51] his own life and durst uneath[52] appear in the King's presence; and even as there were many that stood in fear of him, so likewise stood he in fear of many, in such sort that he began to make those away by one surmised cavillation[53] or other whom he thought most able to work him any displeasure.

At length he found such sweetness by putting his nobles thus to death that his earnest thirst after blood in this behalf might in no wise be satisfied. For ye must consider he wan[54] double profit (as he thought) hereby, for first they were rid out of the way whom he feared, and then again his coffers were enriched by their goods which were forfeited to his use, whereby he might better maintain a guard of armed men about him to defend his person from injury of them whom he had in any suspicion. Further, to the end he might the more cruelly oppress his subjects with all tyrant-like wrongs, he builded a strong castle on the top of an high hill called Dunsinane, situate in Gowrie, ten miles from Perth, on such a proud height that, standing there aloft, a man might behold well near[55] all the countries of Angus, Fife, Stormont, and Earndale as it were lying underneath him. This castle, then, being founded on the top of that high hill, put the realm to great charges[56] before it was finished, for all the stuff necessary to the building could not be brought up without much toil and business. But Macbeth, being once determined to have the work go forward, caused the thanes of each shire within the realm to come and help towards that building, each man his course about.[57]

At the last, when the turn fell unto Macduff, Thane of Fife, to build his part, he sent workmen with all needful

---

50 in manner as it were, nearly   **51 doubt** fear for   **52 uneath** reluctantly, scarcely   **53 make those . . . cavillation** do away with those persons by one fraudulent piece of legal chicanery   **54 wan** won   **55 well near** nearly   **56 charges** expenses   **57 his course about** taking his turn

provision and commanded them to show such diligence in
every behalf that no occasion might be given for the King to
find fault with him in that he came not himself, as other had
done, which he refused to do for doubt[58] lest the King, bearing him (as he partly understood) no great good will, would
lay violent hands upon him as he had done upon divers
other. Shortly after, Macbeth coming to behold how the
work went forward and, because he found not Macduff
there, he was sore offended and said, "I perceive this man
will never obey my commandments till he be ridden with a
snaffle;[59] but I shall provide well enough for him." Neither
could he afterwards abide to look upon the said Macduff,
either for that[60] he thought his puissance[61] overgreat, either
else for that he had learned of certain wizards in whose
words he put great confidence (for that the prophecy had
happened so right which the three fairies or Weird Sisters
had declared unto him) how that he ought to take heed of
Macduff, who in time to come should seek to destroy him.

   And surely hereupon had he put Macduff to death but
that a certain witch, whom he had in great trust, had told
that he should never be slain with[62] man born of any woman
nor vanquished till the wood of Birnam came to the castle
of Dunsinane. By this prophecy Macbeth put all fear out of
his heart, supposing he might do what he would, without
any fear to be punished for the same; for by the one prophecy he believed it was unpossible[63] for any man to vanquish
him, and by the other unpossible to slay him. This vain hope
caused him to do many outrageous things, to the grievous
oppression of his subjects. At length Macduff, to avoid peril
of life, purposed with himself[64] to pass into England to procure[65] Malcolm Cammore to claim the crown of Scotland.
But this was not so secretly devised by Macduff but that
Macbeth had knowledge given him thereof, for kings (as is
said) have sharp sight like unto Lynx[66] and long ears like

---

58 doubt fear   **59 ridden with a snaffle** i.e., reined in. (A *snaffle* is a bridle
bit.)   **60 for that** because   **61 puissance** power   **62 with** by   **63 unpossible** impossible   **64 purposed with himself** resolved, made up his mind
65 procure prevail upon   **66 Lynx** Lynceus, one of the Argonauts, whose
eyesight was so keen that he could see through the earth

unto Midas.[67] For Macbeth had in every nobleman's house
one sly fellow or other in fee with him to reveal all that was
said or done within the same, by which sleight[68] he op-
pressed the most part of the nobles of his realm.

Immediately, then, being advertised[69] whereabout Macduff went, he came hastily with a great power[70] into Fife and
forthwith besieged the castle where Macduff dwelled,
trusting to have found him therein. They that kept the
house without any resistance opened the gates and suffered
him to enter, mistrusting none evil. But nevertheless Macbeth most cruelly caused the wife and children of Macduff,
with all other whom he found in that castle, to be slain.
Also, he confiscated the goods of Macduff, proclaimed him
traitor, and confined[71] him out of all the parts of his realm;
but Macduff was already escaped out of danger and gotten
into England unto Malcolm Cammore, to try what purchase[72] he might make by means of his support to revenge
the slaughter so cruelly executed on his wife, his children,
and other friends. At his coming unto Malcolm he declared
into what great misery the estate of Scotland was brought
by the detestable cruelties exercised by the tyrant Macbeth,
having committed many horrible slaughters and murders
both as well of the nobles as commons, for the which he was
hated right mortally of all his liege people,[73] desiring nothing more than to be delivered of that intolerable and most
heavy yoke of thralldom which they sustained at such a caitiff's[74] hands.

Malcolm, hearing Macduff's words which he uttered in
very lamentable sort, for mere[75] compassion and very ruth[76]
that pierced his sorrowful heart bewailing the miserable
state of his country, he fetched a deep sigh, which Macduff,
perceiving, began to fall most earnestly in hand with him to
enterprise[77] the delivering of the Scottish people out of the

---

67 Midas semi-legendary King of Lydia whose ears were changed into
ass's ears for his indiscretion in declaring Pan a better flute player than
Apollo   **68 sleight** cunning device, contrivance   **69 advertised** informed
70 power army   **71 confined** banished   **72 purchase** advantage   **73 liege
people** subjects, those who should owe him allegiance   **74 caitiff's**
villain's   **75 mere** utter   **76 ruth** pity   **77 began ... enterprise** began
endeavoring to persuade him to undertake

hands of so cruel and bloody a tyrant as Macbeth by too many plain experiments[78] did show himself to be; which was an easy matter for him to bring to pass, considering not only the good title he had but also the earnest desire of the people to have some occasion ministered whereby they might be revenged of those notable injuries which they daily sustained by the outrageous cruelty of Macbeth's misgovernance. Though Malcolm was very sorrowful for the oppression of his countrymen, the Scots, in manner as Macduff had declared, yet doubting[79] whether he were come as one that meant unfeignedly as he spake or else as sent from Macbeth to betray him, he thought to have some further trial; and thereupon dissembling his mind at the first, he answered as followeth.

"I am truly very sorry for the misery chanced to my country of Scotland, but though I have never so great affection to relieve the same, yet by reason of certain incurable vices which reign in me I am nothing meet thereto.[80] First, such immoderate lust and voluptuous sensuality (the abominable fountain of all vices) followeth me that, if I were made King of Scots, I should seek to deflower your maids and matrons in such wise that mine intemperancy should be more importable[81] unto you than the bloody tyranny of Macbeth now is." Hereunto Macduff answered, "This surely is a very evil fault, for many noble princes and kings have lost both lives and kingdoms for the same. Nevertheless there are women enough in Scotland, and therefore follow my counsel. Make thyself king, and I shall convey the matter so wisely that thou shalt be so satisfied at thy pleasure in such secret wise that no man shall be aware thereof."

Then said Malcolm, "I am also the most avaricious creature on the earth, so that if I were king I should seek so many ways to get lands and goods that I would slay the most part of all the nobles of Scotland by surmised accusations,[82] to the end I might enjoy their lands, goods, and possessions. And therefore, to show you what mischief may ensue on you through mine unsatiable covetousness, I will rehearse unto you a fable. There was a fox having a sore

78 experiments trials, hard experiences   **79 doubting** mistrusting
80 nothing meet thereto not at all suitable for that role   **81 importable**
unbearable   **82 surmised accusations** false allegations

place on her* overset with a swarm of flies that continually sucked out her blood. And when one that came by and saw this manner demanded whether she would have the flies driven before her, she answered: 'No, for if these flies that are already full, and by reason thereof suck not very eagerly, should be chased away, other that are empty and felly an-hungered[83] should light in their places and suck out the residue of my blood far more to my grievance than these which now, being satisfied, do not much annoy me.' Therefore," saith Malcolm, "suffer me to remain where I am, lest if I attain to the regiment[84] of your realm, mine unquenchable avarice may prove such that ye would think the displeasures which now grieve you should seem easy in respect of the unmeasurable outrage which might ensue through my coming amongst you."

Macduff to this made answer how it was a far worse fault than the other. "For avarice is the root of all mischief, and for that crime the most part of our kings have been slain and brought to their final end. Yet notwithstanding, follow my counsel and take upon thee the crown. There is gold and riches enough in Scotland to satisfy thy greedy desire." Then said Malcolm again, "I am, furthermore, inclined to dissimulation, telling of leasings,[85] and all other kinds of deceit, so that I naturally rejoice in nothing so much as to betray and deceive such as put any trust or confidence in my words. Then, sith there is nothing that more becometh a prince than constancy, verity, truth, and justice, with the other laudable fellowship of those fair and noble virtues which are comprehended only in soothfastness,[86] and that lying utterly overthroweth the same, you see how unable I am to govern any province or region; and therefore, sith you have remedies to cloak and hide all the rest of my other vices, I pray you find shift to cloak this vice amongst the residue."

Then said Macduff, "This yet is the worst of all, and there I leave thee and therefore say: 'O ye unhappy and miserable Scottishmen, which are thus scourged with so many and sundry calamities, each one above other! Ye have one cursed and wicked tyrant that now reigneth over you with-

83 felly an-hungered fiercely hungry   **84 regiment** rule   **85 lastings** lies
86 soothfastness truthfulness

out any right or title, oppressing you with his most bloody cruelty. This other, that hath the right to the crown, is so replete with the inconstant behavior and manifest vices of Englishmen that he is nothing[87] worthy to enjoy it; for by his own confession he is not only avaricious and given to unsatiable lust but so false a traitor withal[88] that no trust is to be had unto any word he speaketh. Adieu, Scotland, for now I account myself a banished man forever, without comfort or consolation.'" And with those words the brackish tears trickled down his cheeks very abundantly.

At the last, when he was ready to depart, Malcolm took him by the sleeve and said, "Be of good comfort, Macduff, for I have none of these vices before remembered,[89] but have jested with thee in this manner only to prove thy mind,[90] for divers times heretofore hath Macbeth sought by this manner of means to bring me into his hands; but the more slow I have showed myself to condescend[91] to thy motion and request, the more diligence shall I use in accomplishing the same." Incontinently[92] hereupon they embraced each other and, promising to be faithful the one to the other, they fell in consultation how they might best provide for all their business to bring the same to good effect. Soon after, Macduff, repairing[93] to the borders of Scotland, addressed his letters with secret dispatch unto the nobles of the realm, declaring how Malcolm was confederate with him to come hastily into Scotland to claim the crown; and therefore he required them, sith he[94] was right inheritor thereto, to assist him with their powers to recover the same out of the hands of the wrongful usurper.

In the meantime, Malcolm purchased such favor at King Edward's hands that old Siward, Earl of Northumberland, was appointed with ten thousand men to go with him into Scotland, to support him in this enterprise for recovery of his right. After these news were spread abroad in Scotland, the nobles drew into two several[95] factions, the one taking part with Macbeth and the other with Malcolm. Hereupon

---

87 nothing not in the least   **88 withal** in addition   **89 before remembered** already mentioned   **90 prove thy mind** test your intent   **91 condescend** agree   **92 Incontinently** immediately   **93 repairing** journeying   **94 required . . . he** requested them, since he, Malcolm   **95 several** separate

ensued oftentimes sundry bickerings and divers light skirmishes, for those that were of Malcolm's side would not jeopard[96] to join with their enemies in a pight field[97] till his coming out of England to their support. But after that[98] Macbeth perceived his enemies' power to increase by such aid as came to them forth of England with his adversary Malcolm, he recoiled back into Fife, there purposing to abide in camp fortified at the castle of Dunsinane and to fight with his enemies if they meant to pursue him. Howbeit, some of his friends advised him that it should be best for him either to make some agreement with Malcolm or else to flee with all speed into the Isles, and to take his treasure with him, to the end he might wage[99] sundry great princes of the realm to take his part, and retain strangers[100] in whom he might better trust than in his own subjects, which stale[101] daily from him. But he had such confidence in his prophecies that he believed he should never be vanquished till Birnam Wood were brought to Dunsinane, nor yet to be slain with[102] any man that should be or was born of any woman.

Malcolm, following hastily after Macbeth, came the night before the battle unto Birnam Wood; and when his army had rested awhile there to refresh them, he commanded every man to get a bough of some tree or other of that wood in his hand, as big as he might bear, and to march forth therewith in such wise that on the next morrow they might come closely and without sight in this manner within view of his enemies. On the morrow, when Macbeth beheld them coming in this sort, he first marveled what the matter meant, but in the end remembered himself that the prophecy which he had heard long before that time, of the coming of Birnam Wood to Dunsinane Castle, was likely to be now fulfilled. Nevertheless, he brought his men in order of battle and exhorted them to do valiantly. Howbeit, his enemies had scarcely cast from them their boughs when Macbeth, perceiving their numbers, betook him straight to flight; whom Macduff pursued with great hatred even till he came

---

96 jeopard take the risk **97 pight field** full battle **98 after that** after, as soon as **99 wage** bribe, or engage for military service **100 strangers** foreign (mercenary) troops **101 which stale** who stole **102 with** by

unto Lunfannaine, where Macbeth, perceiving that Macduff was hard at his back, leapt beside his horse,[103] saying, "Thou traitor, what meaneth it that thou shouldst thus in vain follow me that am not appointed to be slain by any creature that is born of a woman? Come on, therefore, and receive thy reward which thou hast deserved for thy pains!" And therewithal he lifted up his sword, thinking to have slain him.

But Macduff, quickly avoiding[104] from his horse ere he came at him, answered with his naked sword in his hand, saying, "It is true, Macbeth, and now shall thine insatiable cruelty have an end, for I am even he that thy wizards have told thee of, who was never born of my mother but ripped out of her womb." Therewithal he stepped unto him and slew him in the place. Then, cutting his head from his shoulders, he set it upon a pole and brought it unto Malcolm. This was the end of Macbeth, after he had reigned seventeen years over the Scottishmen. In the beginning of his reign he accomplished many worthy acts, very profitable to the commonwealth as ye have heard; but afterward, by illusion of the devil, he defamed[105] the same with most terrible cruelty. He was slain in the year of the Incarnation 1057, and in the sixteenth year of King Edward's reign over the Englishmen.

[Malcolm Cammore is crowned at Scone on April 25, 1057, creating on that occasion many earls and others of rank. "These were the first earls that have ever been heard of amongst the Scottishmen (as their histories do make mention)." The chronicles also record the death of one of Siward's sons at the battle at Dunsinane, and mention Edward the Confessor's gift of healing the "King's Evil."]

---

103 leapt beside his horse dismounted   **104 avoiding** dismounting
105 defamed brought dishonor to

The second edition of Raphael Holinshed's *Chronicles* was published in 1587. This selection is based on that edition, Volume 2, The History of Scotland, folios 150–152 and 168–176. Some proper names have been modernized: Macbeth (Mackbeth), Banquo (Banquho), Lochaber (Lochquahaver), Duncan (Duncane), Malcolm (Malcolme), Macduff (Mackduffe), Bothgowanan (Botgosvane), Birnam (Birnane), Stormont (Stermont).

In the following, departures from the original text appear in boldface; original readings are in roman.

p. 105 *entered enter   *conveyed conuey   *buried burie   p. 114 *yet the son, by the sonne yet by   p. 119 *her him

Further Reading

Bartholomeusz, Dennis, *"Macbeth" and the Players*. London: Cambridge Univ. Press, 1969. Bartholomeusz surveys the history of the play onstage, focusing on actors' insights into and interpretations of the roles of Macbeth and Lady Macbeth, from the earliest performances at the Globe Theatre through the production at London's Mermaid Theatre in 1964.

Berger, Harry, Jr. "The Early Scenes of *Macbeth:* Preface to a New Interpretation." *ELH* 47 (1980): 1–31. Berger argues that from its first scenes the play reveals "something rotten in Scotland" more powerful than "the melodramatic wickedness of one or two individuals." Focusing on tensions and contradictions in the rhetoric of the early scenes, Berger discovers not the natural unity of Scotland that Macbeth's villainy shatters but a culture riven by fear and anxiety that gives rise to Macbeth's fearful desires.

Booth, Stephen. "*Macbeth*, Aristotle, Definition, and Tragedy." *"King Lear," "Macbeth," Indefinition, and Tragedy*. New Haven and London: Yale Univ. Press, 1983. In the tension between the appeal of Macbeth's play of infinite possibility and the moral categories that must condemn him, Booth finds that Shakespeare's play establishes "dual contradictory allegiances" that test the audience "with mental challenges as demanding as the ones that overwhelm Macbeth." The play has a "double action": the tragic events expose "the artificiality, frailty, and ultimate impossibility of limits," and the envelope of the play itself asserts the "comforting limitation of artistic pattern."

Bradley, A. C. "*Macbeth.*" *Shakespearean Tragedy*, 1904. Rpt. New York: St. Martin's, 1985. For Bradley, *Macbeth* is Shakespeare's most concentrated and terrifying tragedy, in which an atmosphere of darkness broods over the play and is "continued" in the "souls" of Macbeth and Lady Macbeth. Bradley focuses on the psychological makeup of the protagonists and concludes, among other things, that Macbeth "never totally loses our sympathy" and that Lady Macbeth, who would have done anything "to undo what she had done," is "too great to repent."

Brooks, Cleanth. "The Naked Babe and the Cloak of Manliness." *The Well Wrought Urn*. New York: Harcourt, Brace and World, 1947. Brooks finds the central themes of the play articulated in the imagery of clothing and children. Clothing imagery testifies to the play's concern with disguising and denying one's "essential humanity"; references to children recur in the play as symbols of innocence, helplessness, and "the future which Macbeth would control and cannot control."

Brown, John Russell, ed. *Focus on "Macbeth."* London and Boston: Routledge and Kegan Paul, 1982. This wide-ranging collection of recent criticism includes a director's view of the play by Peter Hall, an account of its "language and action" by Michael Goldman, a study of visual imagery by D. J. Palmer, and an essay by Peter Stallybrass exploring the relationship of the witches to the play's social and political vision.

Calderwood, James L. *If It Were Done: "Macbeth" and Tragic Action*. Amherst, Mass.: Univ. of Massachusetts Press, 1986. Calderwood holds that *Macbeth* is "a tragedy about the nature of tragedy," self-consciously countering "Aristotelian principles of wholeness." Focusing on its rhetorical and structural resistances to completion, Calderwood traces the ways in which the play's "dismantling of the structure of action is extended into the political and social order."

De Quincey, Thomas. "On the Knocking at the Gate in *Macbeth*," 1823. Rpt. in *Shakespeare Criticism: A Selection, 1623–1840*, ed. D. Nichol Smith. London: Oxford Univ. Press, 1916. De Quincey considers the "peculiar awfulness" and "depth of solemnity" of the knocking at the gate in the Porter's scene. The knocking ends the "awful parenthesis" in which the murder takes place, and "makes known audibly that the reaction has commenced; the human has made its reflux upon the fiendish."

Felperin, Howard. "A Painted Devil: *Macbeth*." *Shakespearean Representation*. Princeton, N.J.: Princeton Univ. Press, 1977. Felperin sees the tyrant plays of the medieval religious drama as *Macbeth*'s primary literary model. Malcolm and Macduff conceive of their return to Scotland in the restorative moral patterns suggested by this drama, and Macbeth, because of his internalization of the culture's dominant ways of seeing, allows himself to be cast as tyrant. The play, however, repudiates the archaic oversimplifications of its forebears in the very complexity that its characters would deny.

Fergusson, Francis. "*Macbeth* as the Imitation of an Action." *English Institute Essays, 1951* (1952): 31–43. Rpt. in *The Human Image in Dramatic Literature.* Garden City, N.Y.: Doubleday, 1957. Drawing on Aristotle's theory of tragedy, Fergusson argues that *Macbeth* is an "imitation of an action" defined by Macbeth's desire "to outrun the pauser, reason." The play traces the virulent consequences of Macbeth's violation of reason, until we are finally returned to "the familiar world, where reason, nature, and common sense still have their validity."

Freud, Sigmund. "Some Character-Types Met with in Psycho-Analytic Work," trans. E. Coburn Mayne, in Freud's *Collected Papers*, vol. 4, pp. 326–332. London: The Hogarth Press and The Institute of Psycho-Analysis, 1925. In attempting to explain the paradox of the personality wrecked by success, Freud finds in Lady Macbeth an example of one "who collapses on attaining her aim." He speculates that her breakdown as well as Macbeth's brutalization can be attributed to their childlessness, which Lady Macbeth perceives as a sign of her impotence against Nature's decree, and which serves as the appropriate punishment for their "crimes against the sanctity of geniture."

Heilman, Robert B. "The Criminal as Tragic Hero: Dramatic Methods." *Shakespeare Survey* 19 (1966): 12–24. Heilman recognizes the play's "complexity of form" and traces its strategies of evoking sympathy for Macbeth. The play moves beyond melodrama, demanding our participation with the protagonist's "contracting personality." In spite of his brutality and our necessary identification with the forces of order, Macbeth compels our "collusion" with his fate.

Jorgensen, Paul A. *Our Naked Frailties: Sensational Art and Meaning in "Macbeth."* Berkeley and Los Angeles: Univ. of California Press, 1971. Jorgensen sets out the play's "sensational" presentation of "the terrible raw nature of evil" and its effects upon Macbeth. Focusing on the play's poetic texture and dramatic structure, Jorgensen argues that "Shakespeare disturbs us throughout our nervous system, by exposing to each of us what is within us."

Knights, L. C. "How Many Children Had Lady Macbeth? An Essay in the Theory and Practice of Shakespearean Criticism." *Explorations: Essays in Criticism, Mainly on the Literature of the Seventeenth Century.* London: Chatto and Windus, 1946; Westport, Conn.: Greenwood Press, 1975. Knights insists on the poetic nature and thematic organization of Shakespeare's drama, challenging those practitioners of "character criticism," such as A. C. Bradley, whose "mistaking the *dramatis personae* for real persons" is mocked in Knights's title. For Knights, *Macbeth* is a "statement of evil" in which three themes predominate: "the reversal of values," "unnatural disorder," and "deceitful appearance." His analysis of allegedly minor scenes reveals the coherence of "the pattern of the whole."

McElroy, Bernard. "*Macbeth*: The Torture of the Mind." *Shakespeare's Mature Tragedies.* Princeton, N.J.: Princeton Univ. Press, 1973. McElroy finds *Macbeth* the "most completely internal" of Shakespeare's plays, locating the tragedy in the discrepancy between Macbeth's moral intelligence and his amoral will. Macbeth thus becomes a tragic hero not "*in spite* of his criminality but *because* of his criminality"; in his inability to reconcile irreconcilable aspects of himself, "he assumes a tragic dimension."

Paul, Henry N. *The Royal Play of "Macbeth."* New York: Macmillan, 1950. Paul claims that Shakespeare wrote *Macbeth* for a specific performance at court on August 7, 1606, as a dramatic compliment to King James I. In composing the play for this occasion Shakespeare focused on political and cultural concerns known to be of interest to James, and in the "show of eight kings" Shakespeare represented the Stuart succession.

Rosenberg, Marvin. *The Masks of "Macbeth."* Berkeley and Los Angeles: Univ. of California Press, 1978. Seeking to know the play "from the inside, as actors do," Rosenberg uses stage history, comments by actors, directors, and spectators, and critical commentary in a scene-by-scene analysis designed to uncover the complexity of the play's characterization and action.

Sanders, Wilbur. " 'An Unknown Fear': *The Tragedie of Macbeth.*" *The Dramatist and the Received Idea: Studies in the Plays of Marlowe and Shakespeare.* London: Cambridge Univ. Press, 1968. Arguing against optimistic moral readings that neutralize the power of evil, Sanders denies that Macbeth is diminished by the end of the play. He is merely defeated, fighting with remarkable energy and a scrupulous honesty about what he has become. In the face of Macbeth's "fierce brand of nihilism," Malcolm seems callow, his victory over Macbeth punitive rather than restorative and marked "with the disturbing ambivalence of all acts of violence."

Memorable Lines

FIRST WITCH
  When shall we three meet again?
  In thunder, lightning, or in rain?
SECOND WITCH
  When the hurlyburly's done,
  When the battle's lost and won.   (1.1.1–4)

Fair is foul, and foul is fair.
Hover through the fog and filthy air.   (WITCHES   1.1.11–12)

So foul and fair a day I have not seen.   (MACBETH   1.3.38)

. . . oftentimes to win us to our harm
The instruments of darkness tell us truths,
Win us with honest trifles, to betray 's
In deepest consequence.   (BANQUO   1.3.123–126)

Two truths are told,
As happy prologues to the swelling act
Of the imperial theme.   (MACBETH   1.3.128–130)

This supernatural soliciting
Cannot be ill, cannot be good.   (MACBETH   1.3.131–132)

                    Nothing in his life
Became him like the leaving it.   (MALCOLM   1.4.7–8)

                    Yet do I fear thy nature;
It is too full o' the milk of human kindness
To catch the nearest way.   (LADY MACBETH   1.5.16–18)

                    Thou wouldst be great,
Art not without ambition, but without
The illness should attend it.   (LADY MACBETH   1.5.18–20)

                    The raven himself is hoarse
That croaks the fatal entrance of Duncan
Under my battlements.   (LADY MACBETH   1.5.38–40)

Come, you spirits
That tend on mortal thoughts, unsex me here.

(LADY MACBETH   1.5.40–41)

If it were done when 'tis done, then 'twere well
It were done quickly.   (MACBETH   1.7.1–2)

. . . that but this blow
Might be the be-all and the end-all!   (MACBETH   1,7.4–5)

Letting "I dare not" wait upon "I would,"
Like the poor cat i' th' adage?   (LADY MACBETH   1.7.45–46)

We fail?
But screw your courage to the sticking place
And we'll not fail.   (LADY MACBETH   1.7.60–62)

Bring forth men-children only!   (MACBETH   1.7.73)

False face must hide what the false heart doth know.

(MACBETH   1.7.83)

Is this a dagger which I see before me,
The handle toward my hand?   (MACBETH   2.1.34–35)

The bell invites me.
Hear it not, Duncan, for it is a knell
That summons thee to heaven or to hell.

(MACBETH   2.1.63–65)

Had he not resembled
My father as he slept, I had done 't.

(LADY MACBETH   2.2.12–13)

Methought I heard a voice cry "Sleep no more!
Macbeth does murder sleep," the innocent sleep,
Sleep that knits up the raveled sleave of care . . .

(MACBETH   2.2.39–41)

Will all great Neptune's ocean wash this blood
Clean from my hand? No, this my hand will rather
The multitudinous seas incarnadine,
Making the green one red. (MACBETH 2.2.64–67)

What's done is done. (LADY MACBETH 3.2.14)

We have scorched the snake, not killed it. (MACBETH 3.2.15)

Be innocent of the knowledge, dearest chuck,
Till thou applaud the deed. (MACBETH 3.2.48–49)

                    Come, seeling night,
Scarf up the tender eye of pitiful day. (MACBETH 3.2.49–50)

  I am cabined, cribbed, confined, bound in
To saucy doubts and fears. (MACBETH 3.4.24–25)

It will have blood, they say; blood will have blood.
Stones have been known to move, and trees to speak.
                         (MACBETH 3.4.123–124)

Double, double, toil and trouble;
Fire burn, and cauldron bubble. (WITCHES 4.1.10–11)

Eye of newt and toe of frog,
Wool of bat and tongue of dog ... (SECOND WITCH 4.1.14–15)

How now, you secret, black, and midnight hags?
                      (MACBETH 4.1.48)

Be bloody, bold, and resolute; laugh to scorn
The power of man, for none of woman born
Shall harm Macbeth. (SECOND APPARITION 4.1.79–81)

Macbeth shall never vanquished be until
Great Birnam Wood to high Dunsinane Hill
Shall come against him. (THIRD APPARITION 4.1.92–94)

Saw you the Weird Sisters? (MACBETH 4.1.136)

Angels are bright still, though the brightest fell.

(MALCOLM   4.3.23)

What, all my pretty chickens and their dam
At one fell swoop?   (MACDUFF   4.3.219–220)

Out, damned spot! Out, I say!   (LADY MACBETH   5.1.34)

All the perfumes of Arabia will not sweeten this little hand.

(LADY MACBETH   5.1.49–51)

Thou lily-livered boy.   (MACBETH   5.3.15)

I have lived long enough. My way of life
Is fall'n into the sere, the yellow leaf.   (MACBETH   5.3.22–23)

Canst thou not minister to a mind diseased . . .

(MACBETH   5.3.42)

                    Therein the patient
Must minister to himself.   (DOCTOR   5.3.47–48)

I have supped full with horrors.   (MACBETH   5.5.13)

She should have died hereafter;
There would have been a time for such a word.

(MACBETH   5.5.17–18)

Tomorrow, and tomorrow, and tomorrow
Creeps in this petty pace from day to day
To the last syllable of recorded time,
And all our yesterdays have lighted fools
The way to dusty death. Out, out, brief candle!

(MACBETH   5.5.19–23)

Life's but a walking shadow, a poor player
That struts and frets his hour upon the stage
And then is heard no more. It is a tale
Told by an idiot, full of sound and fury,
Signifying nothing.   (MACBETH   5.5.24–28)

Lay on, Macduff,
And damned be him that first cries, "Hold, enough!"
(MACBETH 5.8.33–34)

The time is free. (MACDUFF 5.8.55)

Contributors

DAVID BEVINGTON, Phyllis Fay Horton Professor of Humanities at the University of Chicago, is editor of *The Complete Works of Shakespeare* (Scott, Foresman, 1980) and of *Medieval Drama* (Houghton Mifflin, 1975). His latest critical study is *Action Is Eloquence: Shakespeare's Language of Gesture* (Harvard University Press, 1984).

DAVID SCOTT KASTAN, Professor of English and Comparative Literature at Columbia University, is the author of *Shakespeare and the Shapes of Time* (University Press of New England, 1982).

JAMES HAMMERSMITH, Associate Professor of English at Auburn University, has published essays on various facets of Renaissance drama, including literary criticism, textual criticism, and printing history.

ROBERT KEAN TURNER, Professor of English at the University of Wisconsin–Milwaukee, is a general editor of the New Variorum Shakespeare (Modern Language Association of America) and a contributing editor to *The Dramatic Works in the Beaumont and Fletcher Canon* (Cambridge University Press, 1966–).

JAMES SHAPIRO, who coedited the bibliographies with David Scott Kastan, is Assistant Professor of English at Columbia University.

❖

JOSEPH PAPP, one of the most important forces in theater today, is the founder and producer of the New York Shakespeare Festival, America's largest and most prolific theatrical institution. Since 1954 Mr. Papp has produced or directed all but one of Shakespeare's plays—in Central Park, in schools, off and on Broadway, and at the Festival's permanent home, The Public Theater. He has also produced such award-winning plays and musical works as *Hair*, *A Chorus Line*, *Plenty*, and *The Mystery of Edwin Drood*, among many others.